TURKS AND BRAHMINS

UPHEAVAL AT MILBANK, TWEED

WALL STREET'S GENTLEMEN TAKE OFF THEIR GLOVES

ELLEN JOAN POLLOCK

American Lawyer Books / SIMON AND SCHUSTER

NEW YORK LONDON TORONTO SYDNEY TOKYO SINGAPORE

SIMON AND SCHUSTER
Simon & Schuster Building
Rockefeller Center
1230 Avenue of the Americas
New York, New York 10020

SIMON AND SCHUSTER and colophon are registered
trademarks of Simon & Schuster Inc.

Designed by Laurie Jewell
Manufactured in the United States of America

1   3   5   7   9   10   8   6   4   2

Library of Congress Cataloging in Publication Data

Pollock, Ellen Joan.
Turks and Brahmins: upheaval at Milbank, Tweed : Wall Street's
gentlemen take off their gloves / Ellen Joan Pollock.
p.   cm.
Includes index.
1. Milbank, Tweed, Hadley & McCloy—History.   2. Law
partnership—New York (N.Y.)—History.   3. Lawyers—
New York (N.Y.)—Biography.
I. Title.
KF355.N4P65   1990
346.73'0682'097471—dc20   90-43519
[347.306682097471]   CIP

ISBN 0-671-61221-2

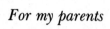

For my parents

ACKNOWLEDGMENTS

THIS BOOK COULD NOT have been written without the help and support of many people.

At Simon and Schuster, Alice Mayhew's insight and guidance helped me shape the story. David Shipley's close scrutiny of the manuscript was invaluable. I greatly appreciated their encouragement as I completed this book.

I probably would not have taken on this project had it not been for Steve Brill, my editor at *The American Lawyer* for ten years. He kindled my interest in the business of law.

Throughout my work, the support of friends and colleagues went well beyond the bounds of friendship and duty. Jill Abramson and the Griggs clan provided the perfect setting one summer for me to write a large chunk of the manuscript. Kathy States provided a patient sounding board for reporting and writing ideas. My spirits were constantly bolstered by Tim O'Brien's good humor.

I want to thank Stephen Adler, Tim Sullivan, Denise Martin, Vittoria Gassman, Leah Rozen, Donna Backer, Larry Backer, Fran Black, Jim Stewart, Rachel Pollock, Dorothy Finelli and Chris Policano for their support, patience, and occasional nagging.

The understanding of editors and reporters I have worked with at *The American Lawyer,* the *Manhattan Lawyer,* and *The Wall Street Journal* was also much appreciated.

Darci Picoult energetically helped me fact-check the manuscript.

I relied on several published sources for Milbank and Rockefeller family history. Two privately published Milbank histories, *Law Practice in a Turbulent World,* 1965, and *Histories of the Predecessor Firms of Milbank, Tweed, Hope & Webb,* 1937, were especially helpful. I also used an interview with Harrison Tweed provided by the Columbia University Oral History Research Office.

For background on the Rockefeller family I sometimes turned to *The Rockefellers,* by Peter Collier and David Horowitz (Holt, Rinehart and Winston, 1976), and Carol J. Loomis's excellent article on the family which appeared in *Fortune* magazine, August 4, 1986.

The revenue and profit figures for Milbank and other firms were taken from *The American Lawyer*'s annual ranking of law firms by revenues. I reported Milbank's numbers for that survey until this year.

Most of the information in this book, however, was gathered during the course of almost 400 interviews with Milbank lawyers, their clients, and others. Over a period of several years, many Milbank partners spent many hours with me, sharing their thoughts and fears about the changes in the firm. I very much appreciate their generosity.

CONTENTS

INTRODUCTION

MY FRIENDS WHO know of my interest in law firms were not surprised that I undertook to write a book about the changing legal profession, but they were surprised that I chose to focus on Milbank, Tweed, Hadley & McCloy. The prestigious law firm, with its roots in the last century, was not an obvious choice. By the early 1980s, it seemed that Milbank, Tweed had been left behind by other large firms like Skadden, Arps, Slate, Meagher & Flom; Cravath, Swaine & Moore; and Wachtell, Lipton, Rosen

& Katz—firms that had ridden the wave of mergers and acquisitions. "M&A" was the practice area that had hoisted the stars of the profession to unprecedented levels of financial success and yes, even glamour. Until M&A became big business, the media had rarely turned its attention to lawyers except to cover big, glitzy trials.

By the mid-1980s, Milbank not only did not glimmer, it was a little down at the heels. The firm was far from ruin. It had long represented the Chase Manhattan Bank and the Rockefeller family—the kind of clients that M&A upstarts like Skadden and Wachtell had coveted when they were young and on the make. But the measure of security provided by Chase and the Rockefellers had caused a complacency at Milbank that had made it easier for younger, hungrier firms to overtake it in terms of size and profits.

Milbank was caught between two eras, a danger zone for even well-established New York law firms. Generations of Milbank partners had come to work each day at their tasteful offices at One Chase Manhattan Plaza, the headquarters of their most revered customer, and waited for the phone to ring with business. It always had. The partners had managed their firm with a sort of nonchalance, a confidence that at the end of each quarter, after Chase and other clients had paid their bills, there would be enough money to pay mortgages on Manhattan's best co-ops, homes in Larchmont, Darien, and Greenwich, and summer retreats in East Hampton, Cape Cod, and Maine.

Finally, a few Milbank partners began to realize they could no longer take their good fortune for granted. All around them law firms were falling victim to internal bickering and the economic realities of a new, highly competitive era. Other established firms, that had viewed prosperity as a given—firms such as New York's Greenbaum, Wolff & Ernst—dissolved. And old-line firms, such as Winthrop, Stimson, Putnam & Roberts and Donovan Leisure Newton & Irvine, seemed on the verge of slipping from the top ranks of law firms.

Skadden, Arps and other relative newcomers had snapped up the hostile-takeover work that some white-shoe firms like Milbank had considered ungentlemanly and too labor-intensive—and these leftovers turned out to be the bread and butter of the 1980s. Meanwhile, routine legal work that firms like Milbank had thrived on was increasingly taken over by in-house counsel—staff lawyers hired by companies to do the work more efficiently and at a lower cost. Outside counsel was reserved for specialized or unusually complex work. It was a trend even Milbank couldn't escape. Chase's legal department—for years overshadowed by Milbank—had suddenly blossomed with talent and skill.

Wall Street was under intense pressure to become more competitive. Investment-banking partnerships like Salomon Brothers, Lehman Brothers, and White Weld were selling out to other corporations or going public. Milbank's legal competitors were revamping their managements to allow them to maneuver more easily in the more competitive climate. While not shedding their partnership structures, many law firms began to borrow management techniques from their investment-banking and corporate clients. They were marketing and watching the bottom line. Some streamlined governance by turning over day-to-day responsibility for running the firm to a cadre of partners vested with enough power to make quick decisions.

More significantly, many firms were abandoning "lockstep," the traditional method of compensating partners according to seniority. These forward-thinking firms rewarded "rainmaking" (the generating of new business) and legal skill with cold, hard cash. And they lured talented outsiders away from other firms with promises of even greater financial rewards.

At stake was the loyalty of large companies that had traditionally relied on these firms for advice. Old line law firms had long ago shed their entrepreneurial beginnings and their partners could not identify with the new hunger with which their clients pursued deals and financings. In the fast-paced 1980s, businessmen needed quick service, up-to-date expertise, and the right lawyer assigned to their work. If they didn't get it, they went elsewhere. Long time relationships were not as important to these clients as getting the job done right. Milbank was not alone in feeling this new pressure. Uptown and downtown law firms were trying to reshape themselves to keep up with the needs of their ever more aggressive corporate clients.

To the Milbank partners, however, the changes in the legal profession were anathema. No fewer than nine partners ran the firm, and they constantly invited the rest of their partners to mull over decisions at Monday lunches at the old-world Down Town Association and in their offices at One Chase. The prospect of marketing themselves made the conservative partners acutely uncomfortable. Abandoning lockstep was out of the question.

This book tells the story of Milbank's awakening: how a group of close-knit men fought to keep their business afloat. It was not a bloody fight. Over the years, the partners had developed an insular, noble culture that seemed in many ways to belong to an earlier century. In a sense they had to battle themselves and their allegiance to a way of doing business that was archaic, even laughable, in the cutthroat world of Wall Street in the eighties.

In 1984 the chairman of the firm committee, as Milbank's governing body was called, reached retirement age, and a new leader was selected. It fell to Alexander Forger to ensure that Milbank made it into the twenty-first century with its reputation intact. Goaded on by a few young radicals, Forger sought to convince his tradition-bound partners that for the first time since the 1950s they had to rethink the way they ran their firm. He prodded and cajoled. In some ways it was like introducing an isolated tribe to the mysteries and complexities of modern-day business. Older partners had to swallow their pride and take clients to lunch. Younger partners awkwardly tried their hand at the power breakfast.

Partners accepted changes they would have found unthinkable only several years before. The firm's client base was expanded. The lockstep compensation system was modified so that big business producers could be adequately compensated. Rainmakers were lured away from other firms. The firm's growth spurt meant that for the first time in Milbank's history, partners were not always able to recognize each other in the corridors of One Chase Manhattan Plaza.

The changes did not come about without trepidation and regrets. The partners were forced to rethink their never-before-questioned belief that partnership was for life. They made decisions that pained every member of the firm. These decisions were based mostly on financial realities, with scarcely a nod to the loyalties that had long glued the partnership together. They ignited such fury among the partners that they threatened to topple the firm's new strategies for the future.

By the late 1980s, Milbank had been transformed. The firm's young progressive partners were elated. Milbank's slide had been stopped. The partners still did not make as much money as some of their counterparts at other top firms, but their compensation was nonetheless respectable. They had good reason to be confident about the future.

But a price had been paid for this new strength and security. Some of the older, conservative men mourned the damage done to the firm's culture. They felt disenfranchised, as if the rules had changed midway through their careers. Even the partners who accepted the transformation felt a bit nostalgic for the old days. "In the sixties, you practiced law and it was wonderful," remarked partner Pete Connick wistfully. "Maybe you got together a couple of times a year and you discussed the profits, if there were any, and associates never talked back and it was jolly."

1

MILBANK
CHOOSES
A NEW
CHAIRMAN

EVERY MONDAY AT half past noon, the partners of Milbank, Tweed, Hadley & McCloy stepped back into the nineteenth century. If at all possible, the partners stopped billing hours and headed for the Down Town Association a block away. The club is a haven for the wealthy Wall Streeter: Windsor chairs fill a somber wood-paneled cavern where members read newspapers, smoke cigars, and sip coffee from demitasse cups in front of a fire. In the dining rooms upstairs, waiters who have memorized the members' secret cravings for dessert tread quietly on the narrow paths of heavy red carpeting that run along the rooms' dark, wood floors.

In a DTA meeting room every Monday, the Milbank partners lunched and casually conversed about client matters and finances. Sometimes the partners would listen to a report from the chairman of the firm committee, the group that oversaw the day-to-day operation of the old-line Wall Street firm. To compensate the partners for their attendance, each received a crisp ten-dollar bill—fresh from the Federal Reserve a few blocks away. The cash was dispensed by Ronald Cullis, the firm's nonlawyer executive director, who briefly transformed himself into a medieval clerk despite his executive experience at a Fortune 500 company. No partner's memory stretched back far enough to recall how this tradition had started.

The Milbank culture was almost a religion. There was a certain sameness to the partners. It was more than their near-identical suits and conservative ties, which took on bird or sailboat motifs when the creative spirit stirred the wearer. The partners cultivated a reserved, aristocratic air—a clubbiness—that was all their own. William E. Jackson, the revered chairman of the firm committee for five years until 1984, liked to point out that Milbank was remarkably free from internal strife and factionalism. Indeed, until 1983, no partner had ever defected to another firm.

Of course there was a dark side to this curial way of life. To be accepted into the partnership elite, lawyers had to make the firm their life. "You really have to love it [and believe] this isn't what I do from eight to five. It's who or what I am. I don't feel like I'm putting on a uniform when I put on my suit and my white shirt and my rep tie. It's like a second skin," explained a former associate. "The Milbank lawyer is the quintessence of rectitude—'We're just better than you. It's not just that we're better lawyers, it's just that we're better as a person in a moral sense.' "

But by the early 1980s, the Milbank partners had reason to question the traditions that had served them so well for over 100 years. Milbank could trace its roots to a firm founded in 1866. For the first time in that long history its status was in danger of slipping. It seemed that the firm had been left behind by national megafirms like Skadden, Arps, Slate, Meagher & Flom and other hyperambitious firms like Cravath, Swaine & Moore and Wachtell, Lipton, Rosen & Katz. These firms had pulled ahead of their competitors by making a big splash in the mergers and acquisitions game, and Milbank had missed out.

Though Milbank was not about to leave its elegant headquarters at One Chase Manhattan Plaza for a less exalted address, there were undeniable signs that the firm had lost ground. By 1984, Milbank, once the country's largest firm, had slipped to twenty-seventh in number of lawyers with 229. With $74 million in revenues, and $24.5 million in profits, the firm lagged far behind relative newcomers like Skadden and Wachtell. In 1984, Skadden ranked first in the country with $129 million in revenues. Wachtell ranked first in profit per partner, a statistic used to compare the profitability of firms with different numbers of partners. Though Milbank had three times as many lawyers and almost twice as many partners as Wachtell, it was far less profitable. Wachtell's profit per partner was $795,000; Milbank's was $370,000.

It was equally obvious that other old, established firms like Cravath and Davis Polk & Wardwell had made the transition into this new, competitive era. Cravath and Davis Polk's profits per partner were $635,000 and $500,000, respectively.

The conservative members of Milbank's partnership refused to see that their firm was increasingly viewed by its competitors as a dusty relic, sustained by its representation of The Chase Manhattan Bank and the Rockefeller family. But a growing number of Milbank partners—some with only a few years of partnership experience—were starting to agitate for change.

This was not a revolutionary cabal. At Milbank, nothing was decided without a consensus. Partners at many firms boast that their firms are democracies. But at Milbank, consensus-building had evolved into a high art, a remnant from a time when the partnership was smaller and more intimate. "You talked your own language," recalled firm-committee member Albert F. Lilley, who was something of a Milbank historian. "People were so in tune with each other you didn't need organization. You didn't need charts. You didn't need objectives. Everything intuitively moved."

If Milbank was going to survive in a more aggressive marketplace, however, its lawyers would have to be pushed toward sweeping changes. And so the election of the new chairman of the firm committee in the spring of 1984 was an especially onerous task. It was to be the start of an odyssey for the firm and its roughly sixty-five partners. The man who would replace Jackson, who had to step down when he turned sixty-five, would be responsible for ensuring that Milbank made it into the next century with its reputation as a premier law firm intact.

Even lawyers frustrated with the firm's lack of direction knew that the new chairman would have to be a master consensus-builder; without a consensus, the partners would balk at any change at all.

There were two contenders for the post, Roger B. Oresman and Alexander D. Forger. Oresman, sixty-three, was the front-runner. A tall, dignified man with prominent features and a penchant for white shirts and bow ties, Oresman was one of only a few powerful Milbank partners whose careers were not closely aligned with Chase, or "the Chase" as it was called by Milbankers. Ever since he had become a partner in 1958, Oresman had wanted a say in the running of the firm. He had assumed a kind of "chancellor of the exchequer" role on the firm committee. Since 1979 Jackson had been the titular head of the committee, but he had conducted himself more as an arbitrator than as an agent of change. Some of Oresman's partners believed that Oresman considered himself to be the power behind the throne.

During Jackson's reign, Oresman was also the committee's most vocal proponent of change. He could be argumentative and dogmatic about his views, reminding his colleagues that strategic planning and thinking about the future were a necessary part of running a multi-million-dollar business.

Oresman's credentials as a rabble-rouser had been proven in early 1984 at a partnership meeting at the Wall Street Club that was still fresh in the firm committee's memory. Jackson had formed a planning committee, a concession to partners who bristled under his staid leadership. Its members were charged with developing a strategic plan for the firm. Shortly before the election, the committee made a proposal that set the partnership reeling. It suggested altering the partnership's lockstep compensation system.

In a "lockstep" system, partners are paid solely on the basis of seniority. There are no bonuses for exceptional work and no penalties for those who do not pull their weight. For the most part, a partner's slice of the profit pie is the same as that of every other member of his law-school class.

For firms without lockstep, divvying up profits is often the year's most wrenching experience. Nevertheless, the partners at Skadden and even at "white shoe" firms had decided that lockstep limited their ability to satisfy stars and recruit outside partners. Raiding talent was a new phenomenon. Partners who generated a lot of business for their firms, and who felt undervalued by lockstep systems, had started defecting to other firms.

For the first time there was a market for senior talent.

But Milbank—saddled with lockstep compensation—did not participate in the partner-swapping game. Though the firm was vulnerable to raids and badly in need of fresh talent, Milbank's partners abhorred the idea of taking in lateral partners. The argument was that "cherry-picked" partners were not imbued with the Milbank culture.

At the Wall Street Club meeting, Oresman suggested that Milbank distribute 90 percent of its profits on the basis of seniority and use the remaining 10 percent to compensate partners according to merit. He suggested about six criteria for measuring performance, including billable hours and client generation. It was only a small step away from lockstep, but for Milbank it was a radical proposal.

The partners were shaken. It wasn't simply the idea of breaking with lockstep that shocked them, it was that they had been unprepared for the proposal. At Milbank, decisions were rarely made before the partnership had mulled over the problem and the outcome was obvious. Even new partners listening to Oresman understood that the partnership would not support a proposal unless there was a consensus. Jacob J. Worenklein, a thirty-five-year-old banking lawyer who had made partner only two years before, saw a drastic need to boost Milbank out of its doldrums. The seemingly gentle young man, who until then had kept a low profile, was unsettled by the planning committee's proposal. He thought the plan did not go far enough, but he also thought it had been presented undiplomatically.

Oddly, the partners who spoke most ardently against the proposal were those who would have likely benefited from the change. Senior real estate partner John C. Nelson, known as Larry, who represented clients such as Gerald D. Hines, the giant real estate developer, argued that Oresman's plan would damage the partnership's collegiality and make it less likely that partners would share their clients. Edward J. Reilly, due to take over the chairmanship of the litigation department from Jackson, was also adamant. Unequal contribution is inherent in the concept of partnership, he told the group. Instead of boosting the compensation of intense young partners like Richard C. Tufaro, who billed well over 3,000 hours a year, make them go home earlier to their families.

The partners were taken in by Nelson and Reilly's ardor, and it was clear that the proposal was doomed. "Between the two of them we were dead," said Worenklein, who supported the plan.

Finally, bankruptcy partner John J. Jerome brought the debate to a halt by moving to table the discussion. A graduate of St. John's University School of Law, and the possessor of a quick temper and a loud voice, Jerome was the antithesis of the Milbank type. He had nevertheless taken to the firm and its customs with the fervor of a convert. Even though he was a successful "rainmaker," or generator of business, he was incensed by the manner in which Oresman's proposal had been presented. "With lawyers you have to have due process. You have to lay a foundation," he later said. "It was the worst way to accomplish a goal."

Even Worenklein, realizing that the abolition of lockstep could not be forced on the partnership, voted with the majority to table the discussion. "I thought [the proposal] was ridiculously mild. I thought it was nothing," Worenklein said. "If people get so upset about nothing, why the hell make a big issue of it."

Later Oresman attributed his committee's loss, in part, to what he described as a "leadership vacuum." He had brought the proposal to the partnership with the blessing of the firm committee. "By the time the proposal got to the firm, a number of members of the firm committee had backed away from it and no longer thought it was a good idea," he recalled. "I thought it was a good idea. Sure I was disappointed but I don't think I wept."

Even though the planning group had developed the scheme together, there was no question that Oresman was blamed for the fiasco. Oresman "was willing to stick his neck out and get beat up," said Ronald Cullis, a staunch backer of the plan. Somehow other supporters of the proposal, like Floyd E. Brandow, Jr., the partner who represented the New York Stock Exchange Inc., escaped unscathed.

Forger, Oresman's one rival, was less controversial but had also been less visible inside the firm for a number of years. He had solid managerial experience. Years before, he had been a member of a precursor to the firm committee, dubbed the "Secret Six" because of its vague mandate to run the firm.

For the past several years, however, Forger's attention had been focused outside the firm. He had served in the prestigious post of president of the New York State Bar Association from 1980 to 1981 and became chairman of the board of the Legal Aid Society in 1983.

Meanwhile, Forger had brought new luster to the trusts-and-estates department, which had been in near-shambles. His representation of clients such as Jacqueline Onassis and Joan Kennedy had given new prestige to the department at a time when the "Brothers generation" of the Rockefeller family (the sons of John D. Rockefeller, Jr.) was dying out and the administration of their wills and trusts was almost complete. Traditionally the trusts-and-estates department had been run haphazardly, only to provide personal service to fabulously wealthy clients. But Forger had committed himself to putting the department on a sensible financial footing.

Over six feet tall and slightly barrel-chested, Forger looked like a leader. He had an authoritative bearing and somewhat haughty smile and could easily have been cast as a founding father. Despite his middle-class background, his partners accepted him as a proper leader. Somehow Forger could be patronizing, easygoing, and tough, all at the same time. He used his voice effectively; he could speak to a room filled with people as though he were having an intimate conversation with each person. And he was perceived as a team player, a man who greatly respected the firm's tradition of consensus.

In mid-1984, a few months after Oresman's proposal was shot down, Forger rotated onto the firm committee and was thus eligible for the chairmanship. He was one of several partners invited to join the committee in a regularly scheduled rotation of its membership. The committee then set about choosing the new chairman. Two other members, Reilly and Worenklein, were strong backers of Forger. And because they represented vastly different constituencies—Reilly was older and conservative and Worenklein a newly minted partner—they were particularly devastating to Oresman's candidacy.

During a series of committee meetings that spring, Forger and Oresman would withdraw from the forty-seventh-floor conference room so the committee could discuss their strengths and weaknesses. The committee members tried to predict how each candidate might meet the peculiar challenge of leading the partners of Milbank, Tweed. In between sessions the members indulged in their strange brand of consensus-building. There was no overt campaigning. Cullis called it "consensus by indirection," and privy as he was to the inner workings of the inner sanctum, even he remained a confused outsider.

Worenklein's recent selection as the firm committee's youngest member had given him his first shot at management. He now threw off the cloak of deference he had worn as a junior partner, and, although he stopped short of electioneering, he became Forger's champion. Worenklein feared that other young partners would be unable to appraise the candidates adequately because they didn't know Forger. After all, Forger had been largely absent from the firm for several years, and as a trusts-and-estates partner, he was isolated. Banking, corporate, and litigation lawyers had little need for his expertise on how the rich should distribute their assets after death. Worenklein took it as his mission to spread the word of Forger's leadership potential to his peers.

The young partner was in awe of the older lawyer. While still an associate, he had responded to a memo Forger had sent out requesting assistance on a state bar task force to reform New York's legislative process. The two had started working together, and Worenklein had traveled to Albany with Forger to lobby for the bar's recommendations. The younger lawyer had been transfixed by Forger's tales of public service and his thoughts about the direction of the firm.

Litigation partner Reilly was also a Forger partisan. Unlike many of their fellow senior partners, Forger and Reilly were from middle-class backgrounds. They had graduated from Yale Law School and joined Milbank within a few years of each other, Forger in 1950 and Reilly in 1954. In contrast to Forger's soothing, almost ministerial demeanor, Reilly spoke deliberately and self-consciously, eyes cast downward. He used a ruler to measure the margins on documents and held them up to the light to check that the watermark was not upside down. Some associates saw Reilly, who was prone to anger, as a control freak. Despite their differences, Forger and Reilly had become close friends early in their careers. Forger called Reilly "Brother Reilly." Reilly joked that he did whatever Forger told him to do.

Like many big-firm litigators, Reilly usually settled his cases out of court. At the time that he was pushing for Forger's appointment as chairman, he hadn't tried a case before a jury for almost ten years. When he did appear in court, however, his aggressive probing of witnesses surprised his colleagues. Perhaps that was why Forger had asked Reilly to assist him on a succession of ticklish, high-profile matters for his wealthy clients. It was Reilly who had convinced a federal judge to cite paparazzo Ron Galella for contempt for not keeping his distance from Jacqueline Onassis as previously ordered. In 1984, he was immersed in preparation for what was to be the largest will contest ever to be tried in New York—the battle over the estate of J. Seward Johnson, an heir to the Johnson & Johnson fortune. Johnson's children, dismayed that he'd left the bulk of his approximately $400 million estate to his third wife, had retained Forger, who in turn brought Reilly in as his litigator.

Reilly, like Worenklein, avoided overt campaigning. Still, he found it hard to believe that anyone could oppose Forger. It was probably the last time Reilly and Worenklein, whose more senior partners would soon regard him as a governance terrorist, would agree on anything.

There were nine partners on the firm committee, and Reilly figured that he had five sure votes for Forger. But for some of the partners on the committee, the choice between Forger and Oresman was not so clear. As the deliberations began, Floyd Brandow, who had supported the compensation proposal, leaned toward Oresman. Two other powerful partners, Francis D.

Logan and Albert Lilley, were tentatively for Forger. As chief counsel to Chase, the man responsible for seeing to the needs of the firm's most important client, Logan had tremendous clout with his partners, most of whom were just a little bit afraid of him. But even Logan had reservations about Forger. They had different management styles: Forger was a compromiser, whereas Logan tended to deal with issues in black-and-white terms and favor more draconian solutions. During the course of the deliberations, however, Logan felt reassured that Forger was the right man for the job.

Lilley, who was very fond of Oresman, was also initially torn. He had been a member of the Oresman group, the cluster of lawyers who served the senior partner's clients, before he struck out on his own to represent clients such as Rockefeller Center. Finally, Lilley came down in the Forger camp because he felt Forger had the right management style for the firm. Forger, Lilley said, is "a consensus-getter and he's also action-oriented. He's forceful in a tasteful way, usually with good humor."

Partners talked among themselves and conveyed their feelings to the firm committee. Many were worried that Oresman's forthrightness and sharpness would conflict with the firm's gentle decision-making tradition. "They thought he would end up with all the marbles," said Cullis. "He was too strong for the culture."

By June, support for Oresman had melted away and it was clear that a consensus had been reached. At a regularly scheduled firm committee meeting, Oresman officially nominated his opponent. Forger was the only nominee. It wasn't even necessary to take a vote because Oresman's name was not even mentioned. "It was never a question of rejecting Oresman and embracing Alex," explained Cullis. "It was just known that Alex was the choice." The decision took only a few minutes, and the group drafted a memo for distribution to the rest of the firm.

2

A NOBLE HISTORY

IN 1984, MILBANK, Tweed seemed to be ricocheting between decades. It had a modern computer system. It oversaw sophisticated transactions for one of the largest banks in the world. And yet at the same time it functioned as though it served a wealthy patron family.

The firm had made the transition from the nineteenth to the twentieth century with ease. But its continued allegiance to an outmoded tradition of governance—and to Chase—put the firm in danger of not making it into the twenty-first century with its prestige intact.

Milbank's story was intertwined with the stories of the Rockefellers and the Chase Manhattan Bank. The firm had been blessed with generation after generation of distinguished partners, all inculcated with the near-sanctity of the Chase relationship. They were gentlemen from the best families, with a wealth of business connections and a sense of public-spiritedness. But in many respects Milbank's financial difficulties, problematic client base, and ineffectual management were an outgrowth of its grand history.

From its birth in 1866, Milbank, then known as Anderson, Adams & Young, was a firm where clients from the upper class could be served by their peers. Henry Anderson, the son of a prominent minister with solid political connections, spent each Saturday morning at Grand Central Station taking care of the Vanderbilt family's business. George Welwood Murray became a partner in 1888. He met John D. Rockefeller through their religious activities, and "Senior" (as Rockefeller would be known to generations of Milbank lawyers) soon retained him.

Many years later, in 1936, Murray found himself on the *Queen Mary*, traveling from England to New York with John D. Rockefeller, Jr., his wife Abby Rockefeller, and their son David, then twenty-one. "Junior," nursing a cold in his stateroom, sent Murray a nostalgic note. At the time, Murray was in his eighties; Senior, ninety-seven, had less than a year to live. "You have always had

Father's fullest confidence and highest esteem, in both of which feelings I have participated completely since the early days of my association with you," the card read. "Father often speaks of you, and as long as life lasts you will be to him and to me a highly valued friend whom we both hold in sincerest affection."

The firm quickly became a haven for Rockefeller in-laws. In 1901 Ezra Parmalee Prentice, married to Alta, Senior's third-oldest daughter, joined the firm. Though he soon left to spend his days in Williamstown, Massachusetts, raising cattle and translating *Treasure Island* and the novels of Sir Walter Scott into Latin, his volumes were given a place of honor in the firm library.

Winthrop W. Aldrich joined the firm six years after Prentice. His vivacious sister Abby had recently married Junior. Aldrich and Prentice were hardly the only recruits with social or business connections. William E.S. Griswold, a partner for eight years, was married to the daughter of John Sloane, whose W & J Sloane furniture company was a longtime client of the firm. In 1921,William M. Evarts, whose father, like Henry Anderson's, was an Episcopal minister and a secretary of the American Board of Commissioners for Foreign Missions, joined the firm. In 1926, William Hale Harkness, a member of one of the firm's significant family clients, became an associate. Retired partner W. Rice Brewster recalled singing "Now the Day Is Over, Night Is Drawing Nigh" with Harkness shortly before they went home many evenings.

In 1921, Aldrich brought Harrison Tweed to Murray, Prentice & Aldrich, as Milbank was then called. Tweed had other connections at the firm. His father was well acquainted with Murray. And the senior Tweed's wife was William Evarts's aunt.

It was no wonder that these lawyers just waited for the phone to ring with business. It was a way of life that passed from generation to generation. Family ties helped cement the firm to clients such as the Manhattan Gas Light Company and Consolidated Gas Company.

What sustained the firm, however, was its relationship with the Rockefellers and their bank. On that score, no one was more important than Winthrop Aldrich. Certainly his sister Abby's fortunate marriage helped his career, but Aldrich was a towering presence on his own. Nelson Aldrich, the father of Winthrop and Abby, was a powerful senator from Rhode Island. Both father and son sported bushy mustaches and claimed to be descendants of Roger Williams, although the lineage was a bit murky. As George Welwood Murray had been Senior's legal confidant, Winthrop Aldrich was Junior's.

"He had a business flair whereas I never did have a business flair," Tweed later recalled. "He had the contacts and the ability. He was as able a man as I ever saw."

The firm's largest client was the Equitable Trust Company, a bank in which the Rockefellers had the controlling interest. The firm represented Equitable in a series of mergers. In 1929 Equitable took over the Seaboard National Bank, partly to acquire the managerial talents of Seaboard's president, Chellis Austin. When Austin died unexpectedly, the family was forced to search for a new chairman. Junior asked Aldrich to assume the presidency of Equitable and he took the job "very reluctantly," Tweed later recollected, "under a good deal of pressure."

With Aldrich gone, Junior worried that his legal power would be dissipated. With the help of Thomas Debevoise, the family's staff lawyer, he tried to rectify the situation by persuading Albert G. Milbank to join the firm. Milbank, a partner at Masten & Nichols, was a tough negotiator and business lawyer not known for his technical skills. A college friend of Junior's, he had done some of the family's work and had been selected by Senior as an alternate executor of one of the family wills. But Milbank, a scion of another great New York family, felt he would be leaving his firm in the lurch if he defected. Finally it was agreed that Milbank's firm, Masten & Nichols, would merge with the Murray firm.

It was the kind of merger a modern-day law-firm consultant would encourage. The two firms shared a major client, the Rockefeller family. The practices were similar and easily meshed. Indeed, Masten & Nichols had represented Seaboard in the merger with Equitable and both firms had healthy trusts-and-estates practices.

Nevertheless the merger started with a rocky courtship and didn't smooth out until years into the marriage. Both firms resented being pushed into the merger by the Rockefellers. They had trouble agreeing on how to allocate profits. After another touchy negotiation, the new firm was named Milbank, Tweed, Hope & Webb. Said Tweed of the merger: "I didn't like it, but I'm a fatalist and it seemed to be fate."

Milbank became the undisputed head of the firm.

He was also senior counsel to the Chase National Bank—as the bank was called after Equitable was merged into Chase in late 1930. Tweed, known to generations of Milbank lawyers for his naked walks down his Long Island beach, turned over much of the Rockefeller-family estate work to lawyers from Masten & Nichols because "Mr. Debevoise and I had not gotten along exactly eye-to-eye, and shoulder-to-shoulder, and this seemed a sensible way to work it out."

Despite some damaged egos, the merger worked. For the next several decades, the firm thrived on its blue-chip customers, led, of course, by Chase and the Rockefellers. The firm's clients also included the Borden Company and the Horn & Hardart Company. In 1938 it was retained by the New York Stock Exchange.

In 1946 John J. McCloy, the only lateral partner to be brought into the firm between 1931 and 1980, became a partner at Milbank, Tweed. Recruiting McCloy was Milbank's idea, but he had the support of Junior and his son Nelson Rockefeller, then thirty-eight, who was part of the political world McCloy came from. A former assistant secretary of war and Cravath, Swaine & Moore partner, McCloy had the kind of big name that translated into extra billings. After less than a year, however, McCloy left to become president of the World Bank, and then high commissioner of Germany. In 1952, Aldrich became ambassador to Great Britain; McCloy replaced him as chairman of Chase in 1953. McCloy was never active in firm management even after he returned to Milbank in 1960. His inclusion in the firm's name was more a marketing tool than a reflection of what went on inside the firm.

Albert Milbank's legacy was an institution that was financially secure and capable of running itself. The firm easily survived his death in 1949. But six years later, it faced its first crisis since the 1929 merger. As was typical of the firm's history up until that time, the problem was not caused by an internal event but by the merger of the Chase National Bank into the Bank of Manhattan, which was founded as a water company in 1799 by a group that included Aaron Burr. The combined banks were renamed the Chase Manhattan. For the first time in decades, the loss of the Chase account was a serious possibility. And the uncertainty of the relationship fed the partners' desire to retain the work—and, ultimately, to continue their own overreliance on Chase.

Wilkie Bushby represented the Bank of Manhattan in the merger, and his firm, now known as Dewey, Ballantine, Bushby, Palmer & Wood, was the bank's regular outside counsel. Bushby's firm was formidable competition for Milbank. It had ties to many of Chase Manhattan's officers. Even though McCloy was the bank's chairman, the Milbankers had good reason to feel insecure about the Chase business.

The merger also came at an inauspicious time. William M. Evarts, who had spent over thirty years serving the needs of Equitable and then Chase, had died the year before. Few lawyers in the firm knew the client the way Evarts had known it. The task of ensuring that Milbank's hold on its prized client was secure fell to Roy

C. Haberkern, Jr., who the senior partners felt would be able to shore up the relationship.

In a firm where seniority was revered, Haberkern, forty, was a young man. And, though he came from a prominent family, the fact that he was a Southerner separated him somewhat from Milbank's other partners. Haberkern was gradually earning himself a reputation as one of the preeminent banking lawyers in the country. Lawyers who worked with him almost inevitably described him as the smartest lawyer they knew. "He may be, from a technical point of view, the best lawyer I've ever worked closely with," said partner Charles D. Peet, Jr., who worked for Haberkern for nine years. "He not only had the most analytical mind and was capable of focusing on the narrowest of details, but he was able to stand back and have a breadth of view and make a judgment in situations that were perhaps ambiguous."

Haberkern was a strong, arrogant man who could display a Southern gentleman's charm. He treated women—his wife Carlotta Haberkern was briefly an associate at the firm—with deference. But he could also be extremely hard to work with. Apparently it ran in the family. Former managing partner Francis H. Musselman remembered talking to an acquaintance who described Haberkern's father as "the meanest, nastiest man in all of North Carolina." When Musselman reported this to Haberkern, the latter responded with gusto: "That's my pappy."

Haberkern pushed associates and partners to their limits. Even as a senior partner he typically worked until nine P.M. on weekdays. "He was not an ungracious person unless he was working with you. He was very difficult to work with, very demanding," said partner Daniel G. Tenney, Jr., who added that Haberkern was regarded with "respect, but a certain amount of, not dislike, fear. He was not close to many people. There was a certain personality conflict between him and a great many people."

"He was really there at a time when we were very vulnerable as far as the Chase Bank business was concerned," recalled Tenney. "Roy just became absolutely invaluable."

Tenney was a member of a group dubbed the Secret Six, a precursor to the firm committee. The committee was, in Tenney's words, "amazingly informal," with "no constitutional" mandate. Much of the Secret Six's attention was focused on Haberkern, its youngest member. The committee's key responsibility was to advise him on the Chase relationship. Governing the firm was of secondary importance.

The reinforcement of the Chase relationship was a long process. In the same year as the merger, former New York governor Thomas E. Dewey became a name partner at Dewey, Ballantine. He was a close friend of George Champion, a senior bank executive who would succeed McCloy as the bank's chairman in 1960.

For years, the Chase Manhattan work was divided between Milbank and Dewey, Ballantine, although Milbank had the bulk of it and slowly increased its share. During the 1960s, Dewey was retained by Chase primarily for specific kinds of work, mostly real estate and corporate-trust matters. Over time, Haberkern won the respect of David Rockefeller, and Rockefeller's promotion to bank chairman in 1967 was good news for Milbank. The firm continued to whittle away Dewey's role, and won corporate-trust work back from the rival firm. By the late 1960s, Milbank's name was again synonymous with Chase within the legal and banking communities.

In the mid-1960s Haberkern succeeded William Gaillard, Jr., as head of Milbank, Tweed. Oresman commented: "It was suggested that since Roy was in charge of such a dominant client relationship, it would be useful to have him as chairman."

For years, Milbank's governance had flipflopped between partnership-wide consensus and the dominance of a small group of partners. Law-firm management was a lot simpler then than it is today. It didn't matter so much that information was not widely disseminated by the Secret Six. Except for the bank mergers, there were few pressing issues before the partnership. There was ample opportunity for discussion of whatever topic was brought before the partnership at its weekly Monday lunches at the DTA. But the broad-based decision-making—the partners called it collegiality and consensus-building—was undercut by Haberkern's power. He had the clout of Chase behind him; no partner could deny that he was the fulcrum of the Chase representation, or that without Chase the firm would be in dire economic straits.

For about twenty years, Haberkern ruled Milbank. The growth of the firm's non-Chase business was put on the back burner; Haberkern ran the firm as though it existed mainly to satisfy the bank's needs. Many of his partners thought that he cared about little else. "I think he equated 'what's good for Chase is good for Milbank' [although] I don't think it's that simple," said Jackson. "He was not blind to other aspects, a man as intelligent as he. But he was certainly aware of the importance of that client."

Haberkern often clashed with the partnership. His campaigns to have certain banking associates made partners were successful, but his demands touched off heated battles. Often—but not always—he was forced to accept the partnership's consensus. The partnership did not follow Haberkern's lead, for example, on the question of opening a branch in London in 1979. This issue launched Haberkern on his final rampage.

American firms had long had offices in Europe, but Milbank partners had felt that foreign offices were merely show business and unnecessary. That attitude changed in the late 1970s, however, when American lawyers staged a small invasion of London, where the developing Eurobond market presented intriguing business opportunities for commercial and investment banks and law firms.

Milbank partners feared they would miss out if they didn't make their move. Chase, after all, had a large London operation. Because of Chase, Milbankers had been generally insulated from market pressures, but they didn't have to be hit over the head to see that, if another firm with a London office gained a foothold with Milbank's top client, it would be an invitation for that firm to make greater inroads into that client's business. Among the Milbank partners there was growing sentiment that it was time to take defensive action.

Haberkern, however, believed that Chase's London business could be handled by English law firms and out of Milbank's Wall Street office. "We could do the work in New York and put it in the mail," he said. "In terms of client service I didn't feel that we had any time advantage at all." Haberkern's general attitude toward firm management was conservative and cautious, and he thought branch offices were speculative.

After a protracted debate, the majority of the partners supported the move, and Milbank opened a branch in London's financial district. It was a resounding defeat for Haberkern. His objection to the firm's entry into the London market showed just how out of step he had become. It was apparent to his partners that the strong-willed chairman was increasingly frustrated with Milbank's tradition of consensus-building. Occasionally he would tell Jackson that he couldn't understand why other partners didn't agree with him.

Shortly after he lost the London battle, Haberkern, who was only sixty-four, retired. He did not ease into retirement by cutting his hours the way most partners did: he moved back to North Carolina to raise cattle. From time to time rumors drifted north that he occasionally left his home in Rural Hall, North Carolina, to counsel Southern regional banks; but he did not reappear at One Chase, even for the annual Christmas bash.

In many respects, the firm Haberkern left behind in 1979 was not the one he had joined many years before. For decades the firm had functioned as a monolith, in part because its partners were all part of the same social class. Milbank's corporate department—banking work was handled by a separate group—functioned without a single leader. Though subgroups run by Oresman and senior partner Richard A. Stark dominated, neither ever tried to take command. When Lilley struck out and formed his own group, it was with everyone's blessings.

But a growing number of Milbank partners viewed the firm's values as anachronistic and potentially devastating if they were allowed to interfere with business. There was a certain ingrained elitism in the partnership that could easily cross the line into intolerance and even discrimination. The firm had begun as the professional home for the sons of aristocratic Protestants. It had slowly changed, but the founders' manners and style were passed from generation to generation. In 1985, about a quarter of the partnership was listed in the Social Register. Most of these were senior partners, including Logan, Oresman, and Lilley. Forger, the son of a manager for a wool-manufacturing company, was not listed. Several younger partners also appeared in the register.

The partnership had diversified: Jews and Italians had become valued partners. But the old-line culture had been adapted for new generations. Among the

45

partners there was always a lingering disapproval of less-than-upper-class values and of lawyers who were thought to display their ethnic backgrounds. It seemed more than a coincidence that a collection of ethnic lawyers—some from less-than-top-notch law schools— had ended up in the bankruptcy group.

Historically, large prestigious firms eschewed bankruptcy practice. In New York and other major cities, small bankruptcy firms had been founded by Jews, who were often excluded from white-shoe firms. But in the late 1970s, as the economy faltered, prominent firms had begun to realize that bankruptcy was a lucrative business. Milbank made a push into bankruptcy early. Francis Musselman led the group in the 1970s, but he only practiced bankruptcy law part-time. The real expertise behind the founding of the group was a permanent associate named Samuel Ross Ballin. Ballin, who joined Milbank in 1922, was Jewish and had earned his law degree at nights at Brooklyn law school. He taught bankruptcy law to a generation of Milbank lawyers, some of whom displayed his primitive-style paintings alongside more expensive art in their offices. Despite his long service and dedication to the firm, Ballin was never granted entry into the partnership. Younger Milbank partners believed that Ballin never made partner because he was Jewish, although Daniel Tenney, who joined the firm in 1938 and for many years ran Milbank's recruiting operation, attributed Ballin's perpetual associate status to bad timing and the needs of the firm at the time when he would have been considered for partnership.

The lawyers assigned to learn bankruptcy at Ballin's knee were cast out of a similar mold. Along with John Jerome, Barry G. Radick, the son of Jewish chicken farmers from New Jersey and a graduate of St. John's law school, was assigned to bankruptcy. Radick was an associate for ten years—two years longer than usual—before making partner. He jokingly attributed his long apprenticeship to Jerome's insecurities about having another partner in the small practice group. But a former associate thought Radick simply didn't fit the Milbank image. He likened Radick's manner to that of a "clothing merchant from the Lower East Side. . . . It was pretty clear he wasn't going to get anywhere until he cleaned that up."

In the 1980s, a Milbank lawyer could recall one of his partners referring to a Jewish colleague as "Seventh Avenue." Another senior partner was so uncomfortable saying the word "Jewish" that he had to awkwardly substitute "Hebrew."

Nevertheless it was clear that the partnership's attitudes were changing. The new talent coming up through the ranks had names like Jay Worenklein, Frank C. Puleo, and Richard Tufaro. With growth and lessened homogeneity came new dilemmas, however. Although even young lawyers used words like *collegiality* and *consensus*, they no longer thought the same way about how the firm should run itself. As Cullis explained: "You were dealing with three generations out. For most of the younger partners, Milbank is a law firm, not part of the family."

Haberkern must have realized that the firm was

reaching a point where its haphazard management would no longer be tenable. A year before he retired, he started looking for a solution. In 1978, Al Lilley, the key partner on the Rockefeller Group Inc. account, received a memo from Haberkern appointing him chairman of a study commission. The appointment took Lilley by surprise. His task was to study the firm's governance and recommend improvements. Also appointed to the commission were Jackson, Forger, stock exchange counsel Brandow, bankruptcy powerhouse John Jerome, and banking partner L. Edward Shaw, Jr.

Lilley and his group interviewed every partner in the firm. They collected a string of complaints. A constant refrain was that the firm committee operated too much in secrecy, and didn't stay in touch with the partnership.

Lilley and his team examined the past for clues as to how the firm's tradition could be adapted to the present. They were looking for an easy rationale for change. Senior partners were questioned about the past, and old memos were dragged out and examined. Then, of course, the group tried to develop a consensus among the partners about how to modify the management of the firm. In April 1980, after fifteen months of work, the committee issued its report. The partners voted on various options and the results "looked like minor changes," Lilley said, "but [these] were really significant in an organization like this."

In their voting, the partners changed the system by which members of the firm committee were selected.

Until then, current members chose new members and most partners didn't leave until they died. The partners decided to put the ten members on staggered, three-year terms. Nevertheless, they clung to some archaic traditions. Most partners were against elections because they saw them as a threat to collegiality. Instead, they decided that the committee would continue to select its own members. The partnership also insisted that its allegiance to Chase and the Rockefeller family be reflected in the makeup of the firm committee. Permanent slots were reserved for the chief counsel to those clients— Frank Logan, who had replaced Haberkern as Chase's legal guru, and Donal C. O'Brien, Jr., personal counsel to the Rockefeller family.

Lilley, forty-eight, was against the creation of those special slots. "I wanted to decouple the firm committee from their relationship with those two clients—a double-edged sword, the burdens and benefits of the close relationship with the Rockefeller family and through them, the Chase," he said.

Lilley's attitude reflected a budding sentiment among the younger partners that there had to be more to Milbank than servicing Chase. Many of the changes, in fact, illustrated a commitment to move the firm in a more modern direction. For example, the partners decided that at least one partner under thirty-nine years of age would sit on the firm committee. The partners also decided that the partner in charge of the Chase account would not be permitted to chair the committee. This was a clear reaction to Haberkern's longtime dominance; more significantly, this signaled a recognition that there could be a conflict between the interests of the bank and the firm.

The work of Lilley's committee proved that the partners were not comfortable with the firm's direction and that elements of the partnership were ready for change. Nevertheless, their progress was stymied; they were unable to make sweeping changes that would have encouraged the generation of new business. William Jackson, who had replaced Haberkern, was a conservative and cautious man. As a member of Lilley's committee, he had tried to keep changes to a minimum. Although he had long felt that merit should play a role in partnership compensation, he never forced the issue.

Jackson was the epitome of a traditional Milbank senior partner: tall, courtly, correct, dignified, Yale, Harvard law. His father, Robert Jackson, was a Supreme Court justice and for years the son used his father's chair from the Court in his Milbank office. The family's home had been Hickory Hill, which they had sold to Senator John F. Kennedy, who had then traded it to his brother Robert in exchange for a house in Georgetown.

Jackson was highly regarded by his partners. During his long career as a litigator he had represented Chase and the New York Stock Exchange. In 1975, he won a nine-to-zero victory in an antitrust case before the U.S. Supreme Court upholding the exchange's right to set minimum commissions for its members. The same year he won another antitrust case before the Supreme Court, which set important precedents governing class actions. Jackson also had close ties to the Rockefellers, particularly David.

But Jackson, in an effort to avoid a Haberkern-style dominance of the firm, didn't put his clout to much use during his tenure as chairman. He called his regime "a reaction" to Haberkern's style. Haberkern had run firm-committee meetings as if they were two-hour audiences; he had not been particularly receptive to debate. "I think that a number of members felt that more ample discussion of issues was warranted," said Jackson. "In my tenure I went quite the other way, probably too far, in encouraging discussion of important matters."

More than ten years into his retirement, Haberkern called consensus a "new and disturbing concept."

Jackson didn't particularly enjoy running the firm, nor did he have the time. During his stint as chairman, he represented Chase in its $300 million worth of claims against Iran and in a separate matter worked with McCloy, David Rockefeller, and Dr. Henry A. Kissinger in their efforts to get permission for the deposed Shah of Iran to enter the U.S. Jackson preferred that work to the often thankless job of management.

Jackson was chairman for five years, and during that period the leadership vacuum that Oresman complained about grew. Firm-committee discussions often lasted for six or more hours. Jackson kept his head down—and his schedule filled with billable hours. It was clear to many partners that altering Milbank's course was impossible as long as Jackson was at the helm. And yet, because the committee was not elected by popular vote, there was no way to dissolve Jackson's government. Some frustrated partners simply resolved to wait until Jackson turned sixty-five and had to step down as chairman.

Perhaps Jackson's single contribution to the modernization of the firm was hiring Cullis. Lilley's committee had recommended the abolition of the management committee, which had overseen the firm's day-to-day operation and its computerization. In its place, the partnership brought in Cullis, who had once been vice president and chief accounting officer with the Fluor Corporation; he also became an ex-officio member of the firm committee. Cullis viewed the partners with bemused detachment, as though they were attorneys from an ancient era and it was his mission to lure them into the present with his stock of business tricks.

Lilley and others felt that hiring Cullis was a major first step in the perception that Milbank had to be operated as a business. "Until Ron arrived at Milbank we had no really competent senior executive in charge of the administrative side of our practice," said F. William Crandall, a tall silver-haired trusts and estates partner. "He sensitized all of us to what makes firms profitable."

In 1982, Cullis made his first attempt at strategic planning by distributing a series of Delphi questionnaires to the partners. Developed by researchers at the Rand Corporation in the 1960s, these questionnaires were intended to bring about a consensus on any given subject. Though they had never been used for law-firm planning, Cullis thought the questionnaires might provide a way for Milbank's confused partners to articulate what they wanted their firm to be. Partners were asked to comment on their work environment, the firm's strengths and weaknesses, and at what rate they wanted the firm to grow. Follow-up surveys, circulated after the partners had discussed the results of the first questionnaire, tried to narrow the objectives.

It was all a bit touchy-feely for the staid Milbank crew. Nevertheless, sixty-four of the firm's sixty-eight partners completed the forms. In late 1982 at a meeting chaired by Jackson, Cullis interpreted the results. Partners feared that they weren't generating enough business, that they had an insufficient number of corporate clients, and that they were too dependent on Chase. They believed there were inequities in work loads and compensation. It was the first time the partnership had articulated their fears and dissatisfactions in a clear and open way.

Tufaro summed up the results: "Milbank did not want to be left behind."

3

FORGER
GETS
STARTED

MILBANK'S PARTNERS
knew something was very wrong, but they didn't know
how to fix it. In the spring of 1984 they looked to Forger
to find a way to meet their ambitious but vague goals.
He was perceived as well versed in the Milbank tradition
but knowledgeable about the mounting competitive
pressures from the outside world. They were relying on
him to steer a course between the management styles of
Haberkern and Jackson and lead them through a rocky
transition to a viable future.

When Forger took over as chairman, he didn't realize how difficult it was going to be to nudge the firm into the increasingly competitive marketplace. The Delphi questionnaires had shown that the partnership knew lockstep compensation could not support the kind of law firm they wanted Milbank to become. But when they had been confronted with even a modest plan to fix it, they had retreated.

Nevertheless, as his reign began, Forger was optimistic. "We have been viewed as stuffy and sleepy," he admitted several months after taking office. "If you don't consider the major changes you're going to be left behind, and we're determined that we are going to be recognized as the preeminent law firm."

Forger talked a good game, but he had no proof that his colleagues wouldn't recoil again if he proposed the lateral hiring of partners, growth, and other changes that would strengthen the firm's economics, but ruffle its comfortable world. He convened his first firm-committee meeting in the same soundproof, wood-paneled forty-seventh-floor conference room that Jackson's committee had used. As usual, clerks had stocked the room with yellow legal pads and black pencils engraved with the firm's name. Forger's first matter of business was to convince the eight other partners sitting around the table that the interminable deliberations that had marked the Jackson era had to end. With so many weighty issues, the committee no longer had the luxury of operating like a town meeting. There had to be a division of labor, he argued, and much of the committee's work had to be done outside its formal meetings.

Comparing Milbank to its competitors, Forger asserted, "We may not shoot as high in a major bull market but we have the stability." His boasts of Milbank's renaissance gave his partners a sense of comfort.

Forger talked of "cross-selling," convincing one department's clients to use the firm's other departments, and "marketing . . . a totally new thing for us." He asked bankruptcy rainmaker John Jerome to take charge of partner services. Forger thought that his colleagues would work more efficiently if their personal-investment, insurance, tax, and trusts-and-estates needs were met by the firm. In the wake of a rollicking Christmas party in 1984 at the Plaza Hotel—Milbank's fiftieth—Forger formed an alumni-affairs committee to act as a liaison with partners and associates who had once worked at Milbank. "We just want to stay in touch with the greater Milbank family," he explained. "That's a ready-made network."

But many of these suggestions were cosmetic. Partner services and an alumni network didn't begin to tackle the firm's real problems. Leading Milbank out of its slump would be more difficult than anyone in that forty-seventh-floor conference room could imagine.

Forger began to develop innovations that were more to the point. He formed a client-development committee to work on a brochure about the firm. Only a few years earlier, such a project would have been unthinkable for Milbank or any of its white-shoe brethren. Donley Communications, a respected public-relations firm, assisted the drafters. When Donley had been hired about two years before, a debate had ensued that one former associate described as the struggle "for the soul of Milbank, Tweed."

In his early days as chairman, Forger also revived discussion about a business opportunity proposed by Worenklein about six months earlier. In a half-hour presentation, Worenklein had suggested that the firm start a consulting affiliate. He saw opportunities in several areas, including energy and real estate. (It was an unusual, though not actually new, idea. In 1984, Arnold & Porter, a prominent Washington, D.C., law firm, had started APCO, a management consulting firm. At about the same time that Worenklein lobbied the firm committee, Davis Polk was also debating whether to start a subsidiary to market computer software, a proposal that was ultimately shot down by the partnership.)

The firm committee had promised to consider Worenklein's pitch—but that didn't mean much. They also had expressed interest in another Worenklein proposal: that the firm buy a coal-generated power plant. Through his budding project-finance practice he had learned of a plant on the verge of completion in the Midwest. The utility that owned it had no use for the $100 million in tax benefits associated with the plant. The price tag: $700 million.

In keeping with Milbank's tradition of nonconfrontation, it had been easier for the members of the firm committee to tell their young partner that they'd think about it than to tell him they thought his idea was a bit harebrained. The power-plant proposal, said partner Richard Stark, "wasn't really considered very seriously."

But Forger was intrigued with Worenklein's consulting idea, which included the possibility that the firm could abandon its hourly rate structure in favor of the more lucrative set fees charged by consultants and investment bankers. Most partners remained skeptical. "I think we should go very slow on that," said litigator Andrew J. "Pete" Connick, early in Forger's tenure. "We're lawyers and I'd hate to appear that we're in the travel business or anything else."

While Worenklein's ideas were rejected, his visionary approach led the committee to ask him to draft a statement of objectives. "Jay probably would have done it whether he was asked to or not," said Lilley, the Rockefeller Group's lawyer. Thus began Worenklein's career as Milbank's chief agitator. He didn't look the part: a thirty-five-year-old of medium stature and then prone to chubbiness, the young attorney appeared harmless. He took a personal interest in almost everyone he dealt with and spoke with warmth about the lawyers with whom he worked. That affection was returned. "I've always loved Jay," said Lilley, who supervised Worenklein as an associate.

The young partner seemed to put extra effort into being a Milbank partner. He had a different background and temperament than the other Milbankers. It seemed as though he fit into Milbank only because he so badly wanted to be part of the firm. He thought about preserving Milbank by looking to its future. He analyzed the competition and thought about his beloved firm's shortcomings. At many other firms, he would have been embraced as a managerial prophet. At Milbank he was deemed a radical. His partners didn't know what to make of him.

Jacob J. Worenklein—called Jay by everybody—was the descendant of a long line of rabbis. His parents survived Hitler's concentration camps and after the war moved to Frankfurt, Germany, where his father headed a rabbinical seminary. Shortly before Worenklein was born, the couple emigrated to the United States, where they lived on the Upper West Side of Manhattan, near Columbia University.

From the beginning of his professional life, Worenklein stood out. Before he could vote he was director of research for Frank O'Connor, the New York City Council president during Mayor John V. Lindsay's first administration. He had worked full time even while in college; his father had died when he was a year old, and he had gotten married after his freshman year at Columbia College.

Worenklein opted for the combined JD/MBA program at New York University. As he approached graduation, he was torn as to how to proceed with his career. He was interested in both public service and private practice. The latter won out, in part because he believed that Milbank was committed to public-interest work. The firm actively supported the Legal Aid Society and represented foundations and museums, largely through its link to the Rockefellers.

Worenklein began defying Milbank's conventions almost as soon as he arrived at the firm in the fall of 1973. Most new associates spend their first few days on the job attending orientation lectures and accepting whatever research projects come their way. Beyond articulating their preferred area of practice, they keep their mouths shut. But as soon as Worenklein arrived, he went in search of Robert R. Douglass, one of a coterie of sometime Rockefeller retainers who devoted much of their lives to tending the family's interests. Douglass had spent much of his career working for Nelson Rockefeller when he was governor of New York.

"I knocked on his door one day and introduced myself and said 'I'd like to work for you,' " recalled Worenklein. After two months went by, Worenklein tried again. Eventually Douglass asked Worenklein to help him represent a consortium of New York State electric utilities seeking permission from the public service commission and the legislature to form a joint venture to build all future privately owned power plants in the state. The proposal was shot down; the legislators viewed it as monopolistic and anticonsumer. But in the course of the project Worenklein soaked up everything he could about the utility industry. He combined that new knowledge with his budding banking expertise and parlayed it into a new specialty—project financing for utilities.

By the time Worenklein took his seat on the firm committee, Milbank partners were beginning to describe him as a "catalyst" for change. He was seen as more than just a provocateur. After all, unlike most of his partners, he had developed a new practice area. Only two years into his partnership, it was obvious that Worenklein had the makings of a rainmaker. And so when he talked about expanding the firm's base of clients, even partners thirty years his senior listened seriously, if not always happily.

Worenklein devoted a chunk of the summer of 1984 to his memo outlining the firm's broad objectives for the future. He made a few very specific proposals, but despite its broad strokes, the six-page, single-spaced memo was a revolutionary manifesto. Its call for "growth and diversification" became a rallying cry for Milbank partners eager to restructure the firm.

In the 1970s, the firm committee had implemented a de facto zero-population-growth strategy. The firm had since grown haphazardly. Worenklein called for the rapid increase of the ranks both through law-school recruiting and lateral hiring. He also pressed for geographical expansion. Since Milbank specialized in the representation of financial institutions, he argued, it had to be present in the major money capitals of the world. Branch offices had always been a ticklish issue. Chase had promised the firm work in Hong Kong, where Milbank had an office. The firm also had moved to Tokyo, where it had a unique advantage because the Japanese were willing to allow partner Isaac Shapiro, who grew up in Japan, to practice there despite the nation's prohibition against most foreign lawyers. The move to London had been inspired by the need to defend the Chase turf.

But Worenklein's strategic plan seemed especially

risky. He suggested the firm open an office in Los Angeles. With the exception of a few large firms such as O'Melveny & Myers and Gibson, Dunn & Crutcher, the Los Angeles legal market had been viewed by many New Yorkers as a backwater. But in recent years the city had become the American focal point for what was now called the Pacific Basin. Moreover, Michael R. Milken of Drexel Burnham Lambert had generated thousands of hours of legal business for Skadden's L.A. office.

For years Milbank had toyed with the idea of a San Francisco office, in part because David Rockefeller had significant real estate holdings there. But the partners decided they didn't have enough business in San Francisco to justify the move. Worenklein's proposal to open a Los Angeles office, however, was a far more controversial idea. There was no magnet for Milbank in the form of the Rockefellers nor their bank. He argued that if Milbank saw itself as a premier financial-services law firm it had to be in an emerging financial center. The clients would have to be generated by the lawyers who resided in the office.

In his plan, Worenklein had also suggested that the firm relied too heavily on too few clients. In 1984, Chase, Milbank's largest client, had accounted for about 40 percent of the firm's billings. If the work evaporated, the firm would have a tough battle to survive, let alone remain in the top tier of New York's legal community. It was unlikely that Chase would sever the tie with Milbank or fall prey to a takeover; nevertheless, the partners worried about their reliance on the bank.

Worenklein made some suggestions. Use the banking practice as a springboard into the representation of
other financial services, he urged. In particular, he targeted investment banks. For a firm that had avoided the
representation of smokestack industries in favor of financial-services companies, investment banks had become a must.

This was a touchy point. Milbank had missed the
mergers-and-acquisitions boom. The firm had not done
much better in public-securities offerings. Traditionally,
Milbank represented Long Island Lighting Company's
underwriters and, of course, it handled Chase's stock
offerings. It had handled any number of debt offerings
for clients, including $400 million worth for the National
Rural Utilities Cooperative Finance Corporation, an
Oresman client. And yet it had captured little invest-
ment-bank underwriting work.

The implications of Worenklein's message dis-
turbed the elders on the firm committee. Even Lilley,
the pragmatist, was skeptical about some of Worenklein's proposals. "Jay tends to deal more in generalities
and assume that if we just believe in the dream and move
in that direction things will come true," he said. "The
dominant theme was money. Money isn't all that important to me. . . . Money, more money was the theme.
As we would get into the specifics, the answers weren't
coming back to me from Jay."

It fell to Forger to chip away at the partnership's
skepticism. His partners' reservations, for the most part,
were not irrational: they were based, in large measure,

on the peculiar economics of the firm and its reliance on its key clients. Forger slowly convinced the partnership that they would not be risking key client relationships if they became more independent of those great institutions.

For example, taking up Worenklein's challenge to go after the work of investment banks required the partnership to acknowledge its unfounded fear of alienating the New York Stock Exchange. Because of its relationship with the exchange, which began in 1938, Milbank had traditionally avoided representing investment banks for fear it would run into conflicts of interest. In the 1940s and 1950s, that potential had indeed existed, because the stock exchange had then played a greater role in the regulation of its members' firms. Until the 1950s, Milbank had represented Bache (since acquired by Prudential), but because of a single conflict involving Bache and the exchange, the senior partners had decided to resign from the account. After the 1950s, the exchange's role became less intrusive as the government's policing efforts increased—but Milbank remained cautious. Over the years, the partnership's fears created severe and damaging limitations on the firm's client base.

Partner Floyd Brandow, counsel to the exchange, said, "With the aid of hindsight we wish we had not avoided it. We almost studiously avoided the representation of investment banks and their underwriting activity."

Forger also had to contend with his partners' aversion to the firm's growth. At one firm-committee meeting, Worenklein told colleagues that to reduce the firm's reliance on Chase by half, the firm would have to double its size to 600 lawyers in five years. The percentage of the firm's revenues attributable to the bank would then hover around 20 percent—considered to be a healthier percentage by law-firm management consultants. According to Forger, the committee's response was, "That guy's crazy."

Forger knew, however, that to improve the bottom line, the firm needed more associates. The problem was that Milbank had paid little attention to leveraging—the ratio of associates to partners—which is one of the few undeniable keys to law-firm profitability. Associates, who put in grueling days grinding out billable hours while the partners generate business, are the firm's moneymakers. They do not share profits. So the higher the ratio of associates to partners, the more profitable the firm will be.

In 1984, Cravath had four fewer lawyers than Milbank, but its profits per partner were about $635,000 to Milbank's approximately $370,000. There were many reasons for the gap, but one was that Cravath's strategy was to admit very few associates to the partnership. Cravath's ratio of associates to partners was 3 to 1. Skadden, with 428 lawyers in 1984, also kept an eye on its ratio, which was roughly the same as Cravath's.

Until Cullis arrived in 1980, no one at Milbank even thought about leveraging. When he discovered the firm's ratio to be 1.9 to 1, he immediately began trying to convince the partners, who hoped to keep Milbank's atmosphere intimate, that they had to hire more law-school graduates. By 1984, the ratio had improved to about 2.5 to 1.

Toward the end of the summer, Worenklein distributed a draft to Forger and the other members of the committee. At a series of meetings in the summer of 1984, Forger made sure that the committee members aired their fears and reservations about Worenklein's "growth and diversification" plan. Worenklein was then sent off to revise his draft, and the committee approved it for presentation to the partnership. Then the committee members talked with their constituents, the other partners, to build a consensus. Forger won the support of Jackson. If Jackson, a keeper of the Milbank ethic, supported the memo, it would be easier for his partners to accept it. In September, the full partnership voted to adopt the plan.

What was left was implementation. Members of the committee and other partners were assigned to draft what one partner called "sons of growth and diversification." Logan evaluated the potential of new and existing foreign offices. Worenklein looked into the possible move to Los Angeles.

To pinpoint areas for potential business development, a department-by-department review was ordered. In an attempt to follow the management-by-objective approach used by many corporations, committee members made the rounds of partners in late 1984 and early 1985 to talk with them about their practice. But little came from the reviews, and all the discussion and planning seemed to result only in more discussion and planning.

In a succession of firm-committee meetings, Worenklein waged war against his partners' caution and conservatism. Sometimes it seemed that the more he argued, the more opposition he had to overcome. He wanted to "change the basic thrust of the practice—put us into the absolute mainstream of investment-banking practice, have Milbank, Tweed a household name in big-ticket M&A activity [like] Skadden," Lilley complained.

Ed Reilly, the firm committee member who had replaced Jackson as chief of litigation, was even more disconcerted. He had always detested administrative tasks, and suddenly found himself in the thick of firm and department management. Reilly was far more interested in the contest over J. Seward Johnson's will. When financial reports arrived on his desk in envelopes reserved for confidential communication among partners he tossed them into the wastebasket.

Indeed, the only administrative task Reilly had ever enjoyed was the redecoration of the firm's offices in the late 1970s. The assignment had been perfect for the meticulous Reilly, who was concerned about the wood paneling for the firm's corridors and reception areas. He had selected English brown oak, a medium-toned, rich-looking wood, much of which came from a single tree that had been chopped down seventy miles north of London. Workmen had wetted down unfinished slices of the tree—called fletches—so that Reilly could examine their texture, color, and imperfections. The total cost of installing the wood, which must be periodically refinished and oiled: $3.5 million.

The results were stunning. New associates, fresh from the interview circuit, couldn't help but note that Milbank had one of the best-looking offices in New York. Upstairs, Cravath had made a mockery of its space by installing fake antique fixtures. Downstairs, the lawyers in Chase's legal department contended with dirty fingerprints on white walls. But when they took the elevator up to Frank Logan's forty-eighth-floor office at Milbank, they walked through one of the largest and most elegant reception areas in New York's legal kingdom, past sweeping views of New York harbor and through Milbank's contemporary but dignified hallways lined with art carefully selected by an Oresman-led group of partners.

Reilly did his best to ensure that the offices didn't lose the gracious look he'd worked so hard for. Secretaries and associates were instructed not to pile files and books on the ledges that separated the secretarial workstations from the lawyers' offices. He even demanded that Worenklein reposition his desk so that visiting clients didn't look directly into the glare of the window.

When Ron Cullis arrived, he was appalled to find that a senior partner who billed his time out at more than $200 an hour was devoting so much of his time to interior decorating. It was with some difficulty that he finally wrested control of it away from the stubborn senior partner.

Reilly was a traditionalist. Often he remained silent

at firm-committee meetings. On occasion, however, he exploded. "He and I had the most vociferous debates," Worenklein said. For Reilly, businesslike management was secondary to serving the needs of existing clients. It was almost as though he felt that the partners were betraying their clients by thinking about their own needs. "The client came first, second, third, fourth, fifth, and the firm sixth, seventh, eighth, and ninth," said Worenklein, describing Reilly's attitude. He recalled Reilly explaining to the committee that he viewed "Milbank as a little gem that needs to be polished and put in a little bag in the drawer."

Reilly thought the "growth and diversification" memo was "very imaginative." He remarked that it was "very healthy to have someone take a different look at ourselves . . . from a different perspective." But he didn't buy what he read and heard. He wanted to keep Milbank small. "My concern is that in the process of diversifying and growing in both numbers and geographical location, that we would not necessarily meet our obligations to our present clients," he said.

Reilly was especially distressed by the prospect of geographical expansion. He worried that clients would suffer from a lack of efficiency. He feared the erosion of the partnership's precious collegiality. Although Reilly, an avid sailor, joked that he'd move to Los Angeles "if they would get me a slip at Marina Del Rey," he found Worenklein's dream of a Los Angeles outpost particularly unappealing. "I don't think you can function efficiently or competitively with a dozen New York lawyers," he argued. "You have to bring in significant numbers, and when you do, that's no longer the same firm you thought you had. It isn't a question of good or bad, it's a question of changing the character of the firm. Some people think you have to do [that] to compete. I don't think so."

At committee meetings, Reilly described what he called his "philosophy about what a law firm ought to be. My principal emphasis was [that] New York is still the financial capital of the world." Reilly even had misgivings about the firm's long-planned launch of a small office in Singapore, an important oil-financing center where Chase had an office. "I hated to see someone like [partner] David C. Siegfried shipped off to Singapore," he said.

But Worenklein was making headway. Slowly, he gathered support for the Los Angeles office from two powerful partners on the committee, Forger and Logan. As head of banking, Logan agreed that Los Angeles was a natural West Coast beachhead. Logan was a convert to the theory that the Pacific Basin would prove to be a source of significant business. With offices in place in Tokyo, Hong Kong, and Singapore, he felt, a West Coast presence would complete Milbank's Pacific Basin constellation. A trip to Los Angeles, where he met with potential clients and competitors, helped convince him of the move's feasibility.

Worenklein's efforts to push the firm into the world of mergers and acquisitions backfired, however. In part it was a cultural problem. Martin Lipton and Joseph H.

Flom, the two legal legends of M&A, had pushed Wach-tell, Lipton and Skadden, Arps into the limelight. Take-over specialists were aggressive on behalf of their clients, and competitive even with their own partners. Skadden's lawyers fought to beat each other into the office in the morning. The Milbankers in no way aspired to that kind of aggressiveness or the vast numbers of troops a take-over practice requires.

Worenklein, however, didn't seem to get the mes-sage that his fellow committee members weren't ready to turn their firm into a hard-driving Skadden, Arps or Wachtell, Lipton. He kept coming up with increasingly absurd proposals. In his first year on the committee, he proposed two possible mergers that sent the commit-tee—and then the firm, when the gossip spread—into gales of laughter. Why not inquire whether Wachtell would like to merge? he had suggested. Perhaps Wach-tell would be interested in adding a financial-services component to its superior M&A capability, Worenklein said. And when that idea was shot down, he suggested merging with Cleary, Gottlieb, Steen & Hamilton, whose clients included Salomon Brothers, Inc. The suggestion wasn't even taken seriously.

Forger called Worenklein "a refreshing spirit" and a "visionary." But the young partner's credibility with the partnership was suffering. He managed to inspire unusual candor in his typically reserved partners. After he made the merger proposals, one committee member laughingly said, partners thought he was "bonkers, ab-solutely off his rocker."

"They would hoot Jay out of the place," remembered Forger. "A lot of the old-timers [joked], 'That's Jay, he's on pot or something.' " Milbank's 1985 Christmas show, produced by partner Peter Windley Herman, spoofed Worenklein's "manifest destiny" philosophy. He was portrayed advocating a Milbank, Tweed branch on the moon, to the tune of "Fly Me to the Moon."

The more conservative partners, even some who brought in business, despised Worenklein's radical views. One of the partners making efforts to cultivate new corporate contacts was Guilford W. Gaylord, a member of partner Richard Stark's practice group, which appeared to be running out of steam as its namesake got older and its clients were acquired by other companies. "Going out and getting business has not been a high-priority item around here for many, many years," admitted Gaylord. "It wouldn't be now except for 'growth and diversification.' " He found Worenklein's campaign offensive, and a threat to the firm's reputation for quality. He disdainfully called *growth and diversification* "buzzwords."

"I hate images over substance. I hate that. I hate buzzwords. They're just word solutions," he said angrily. "It's almost sickening, isn't it? It doesn't mean anything. Foreign offices—even L.A.—can come about without those buzzwords."

Finally Worenklein became sensitive to his growing reputation. He became aware that banking partner Frank Puleo, the other young member of the committee, seemed to command greater respect—or at least was considered more dependable—than he. Puleo, who spent most of his time working for Chase, was also progressive, but in a more measured way. "Nobody would ever say that Frank Puleo would have an office on the moon," Worenklein complained.

Forger's first year and a half in office had produced mixed results. The downside was that there had been no obvious improvement in the firm's condition. It remained vulnerable to competition. Milbank still had no Los Angeles office and still relied too heavily on Chase. No new rainmakers with significant business had been brought in from the outside. Although Forger had talked about bringing in a municipal-finance or communications practice, nothing had happened. There was no new flurry of investment-banking business—M&A or otherwise.

Nevertheless, the nine members of the firm committee had agreed on something key—that they were an ineffectual bunch. Forger's exhortation that committee meetings must not be mired in discussion had not been heeded. "It continued to be that way for a year," he said, "and I nearly lost my mind." There was no question that the firm's governance involved too many people. It needed an overhaul. Most of the partners on the committee—with the exception of John Jerome—were also convinced that lockstep compensation wasn't working. In order to bring in strong partners with business, they believed, lockstep had to be "modified"— a word they thought would be reasonably palatable to their partners. Puleo was assigned to write a proposal on revamping the firm's management. Forger began to sketch a plan for modifying lockstep.

But Forger's greatest success during that year and a half was real, though more subtle: without flying in the face of Milbank's traditions or ignoring its noble history, he had convinced his partners that the firm's problems would not go away without their intervention. He could not have done it without Worenklein. For Forger, desperately trying to see past his fellow senior partners' reticence about change, Worenklein was a scouting party sending word back about the future. Compared to his young partner, Forger always seemed temperate and safe.

Forger was slowly preparing the partnership for change. Despite Lilley's assertions to the contrary, believing in the dream did make a difference. In the year after the "growth and diversification" memo was distributed, partners began thinking about generating clients and running their law firm in a more businesslike fashion. Without the benefit of their seniors' example, Milbank's young turks began wining and dining corporate executives and bringing in new clients.

Slowly, Milbank's partners began to realize that their future did not rest solely on their relationships with Chase and the Rockefellers. The partners began to understand that they could not rely on those clients. If they prepared for the changes instead of fighting the inevitable, they would make it into the next century with their reputation intact.

4

THE
ROCKEFELLERS

IN EARLY 1985, WHEN Forger had not yet been chairman for a year, Milbank's partners had to face immutable evidence that even their relationship with the Rockefeller family was entering a new era. After a short negotiation, the family bought the land beneath Rockefeller Center, the midtown Manhattan symbol of its prominence through three generations. They acquired the land from Columbia University, which had previously leased the land to the Rockefellers.

The deal, a happy occasion for the family, was bittersweet for Milbank. The partners were, of course, pleased that their client had accomplished a longtime goal of acquiring the property. But they were not so pleased that the family had done the deal without involving the firm. It was one of the first major deals the family had made without Milbank at its side.

The agreement had been made quickly. Rockefeller Group Inc., the corporate entity responsible for the family's business, had learned that Columbia was negotiating to sell the land to First Winthrop Corporation of Boston. For RGI, the prospect of dealing with a new—possibly less amiable—landlord was not appealing. RGI president and chief executive officer Richard A. Voell met Columbia president Michael I. Sovern for drinks in the Rainbow Room, the elegant restaurant atop 30 Rockefeller Plaza. The hardest issue to negotiate was money. But the two presidents finally agreed on a $400 million price tag. The family would pay the highest amount ever for a single piece of land.

Once the price was resolved, the deal was relatively simple to structure. Milbank had been involved in previous aborted purchase attempts of the land, but there seemed no reason to summon the firm to the bargaining table—or to pay its hourly rates. The Rockefeller family—or rather RGI—turned to its general counsel, Jonathan D. Green, to negotiate the land deal. Green and another in-house lawyer worked opposite a much larger team for Columbia University. The university used two in-house lawyers, two partners and six other lawyers from a powerful law firm, Weil, Gotshal & Manges. Charles A. Goldstein, one of the city's most prominent real estate lawyers, also worked on the deal. It took only a few days to complete.

Peter Herman, a young Milbank partner who advised the Rockefellers on real estate matters, felt that the transaction was not difficult, and that Milbank's expertise was not needed. "That may sound like sour grapes and it may be," he admitted. "We would have liked that—the number-one real estate client over many generations was Rockefeller Center."

Five years earlier, Milbank's absence from such a Rockefeller deal would have been unthinkable. The firm had been intimately involved in the birth of Rockefeller Center. In 1929, John D. Rockefeller, Jr., had leased from Columbia 11.7 acres bordered by Fifth Avenue and the Avenue of the Americas and Forty-eighth and Fifty-first streets. In the early nineteenth century, New York State had granted Columbia the land when it was far north of Wall Street and the rest of what was then the heart of New York City.

Rockefeller was attracted to the property because the Metropolitan Opera Company planned to build a new theater on the site. He agreed to pay about $3 million annually for twenty-four years. But after the stock-market crash later that year, the Metropolitan pulled out of the project. Forced to come up with an alternative scheme, Rockefeller decided to build what would ultimately be called Rockefeller Center.

First he had to acquire the leases and subleases on

the land and remove the tenants. The property was covered with tenements, many of which housed speakeasies and bordellos. And so Rockefeller asked Milbank to do something about the mess.

Milbank turned to permanent associate Sam Ballin, who went to work clearing out the residents and overseeing the necessary court proceedings. It turned out to be an arduous task. One woman refused to leave the premises and climbed into her bathtub. Ballin called the sheriff's office and she was soon banished. In a privately published history of the firm, Ballin's tenant relations were described as "tough but merciful to those who confessed the error of their ways. Means were not always orthodox, but in the end . . . sin sought safer shelter elsewhere." Eventually, the Milbank team acquired 250 leases and subleases.

By 1985, however, when Ballin was eighty-three years old and retired, the Rockefellers had no need to hire Milbank even for a sensitive task involving Rockefeller Center. Like many corporations in the 1980s, the family had increased their reliance on in-house lawyers. Hourly rates were skyrocketing and executives, especially at large companies, realized that it was cheaper to bring lawyers in-house, and assume their salaries and overhead costs, than to pay outside firms. For these companies, there was a lucky confluence of events. Generations of large-firm associates had viewed partnership as a good bet at the end of their apprenticeships—but in the late 1970s, firms were taking in huge classes, and anointing very few associates with partnership. There was thus a surplus of talented, highly trained young lawyers on the street, and they were gobbled up by companies beefing up their in-house legal departments.

The younger generation of general counsel were too ambitious and savvy to be left out of important decision-making. They were usually smart enough to prove to the senior officers in their companies that quality work could be done at a cheaper price in-house. Choosing lawyers, not law firms, became the aim of general counsel. Traditional relationships were relinquished as general counsel selected outside lawyers for specific tasks. A general counsel seeking to control costs figured out what work—no matter how sophisticated—was required by his company on a routine basis. Those matters were brought in-house. Outside counsel was reserved for complex, cutting-edge work or deals that required large numbers of lawyers.

Jonathan Green, the Rockefeller Group's general counsel, was hired by the Rockefellers in 1980, when he was thirty-four years old. As an associate at Thacher, Proffitt & Wood, a respected midsize Manhattan firm, Green had worked on the development of the Continental Building on South Street. Thacher, Proffitt had represented Continental Insurance Company. Also involved in the development of the building was Rockefeller Center, represented by Al Lilley and other Milbank lawyers. Green, then an up-and-coming young associate, impressed certain Rockefeller-family executives, and they went after him with Milbank's blessing. Although Green replaced Richard Norwood, a onetime

Milbank associate, the firm wasn't worried that the young lawyer might supplant the firm in a serious way.

By 1983, Green had been promoted to vice president, general counsel, and secretary of RGI. Although he often relied on Lilley and those who worked under the corporate partner at Milbank, Green was fully capable of handling a big real estate deal—such as the purchase of the Rockefeller Center property—on his own. RGI's lawyers, he said, "generally try to be the lead in any transaction."

Green's attitude about retaining outside counsel was further proof that the Rockefellers would never again be as steady or predictable a source of business for the firm. The traditions that bound the family to Milbank meant little to Green. As far as he was concerned, there was no reason he couldn't use other firms as well. "I really don't think there's any one firm that we'd consider our lawyers," he said. Green had high praise for Milbank's work on complex matters and he said that he always got "the feeling that Milbank has our best interests in mind." But he added, "any service provider should feel they have to compete for your business."

During the course of the century the relationship between Milbank and the Rockefellers had evolved as the family's personal and business preoccupations had changed. The 1985 purchase of the land and other events of the mid-1980s were further proof that Milbank was going to have to adjust to a different kind of relationship with the family.

With each year, the family ran itself more like a

business and less like a collection of individuals with personal loyalties to their counselors. The passing of the "Brothers generation"—David and Laurance were the only ones left—and the coming of age of the "Cousins" and "Fifth Generation" (as Junior's grandchildren and great-grandchildren were called), meant that the interests of the family were diluted. There were no great entrepreneurial talents among the new generations to supply new projects for Milbank's lawyers to facilitate and document.

Some Milbankers hadn't been able to see that profound changes were coming, partly because of the way the account had historically been managed. The firm did not account for the Rockefeller business as a single client, and therefore did not generate statistics to show what percentage of its revenues were attributable to the family. Partners assumed it accounted for well under 10 percent of the firm's billings. And more significantly, perhaps, Milbank did not take the arrival of new in-house lawyers as a sign that they might lose some control over the relationship. The family had always had in-house lawyers. The difference was that now Milbank was unable to control them.

The Rockefellers' in-house lawyers had always had an impact on the lives of the Milbank lawyers who served the family. Earlier in the century, Junior had relied on Thomas M. Debevoise, who devoted his professional life to the family. When Debevoise needed outside help, he called on Milbank. When he retired, Debevoise wanted Patterson, Belknap, Webb & Tyler partner Vanderbilt

81

Webb named as his replacement. But Nelson Rockefeller successfully pushed for John Lockwood to be the family's lawyer in personal matters, in what Lockwood later described to Peter Collier and David Horowitz, authors of *The Rockefellers,* as a "squeeze play."

John E. Lockwood, who had clerked for Supreme Court Justice Oliver Wendell Holmes, Jr., had ended up at Milbank (then called Murray & Aldrich) on the advice of Debevoise, his father's friend. He had started advising Nelson, whom he referred to as "my longtime friend and client," soon after the young Rockefeller left for Dartmouth. Nelson "needed someone his own age" to turn to for advice, said Lockwood.

Lockwood gave up his Milbank partnership to follow Nelson to Washington, D.C. As coordinator of the Office of Inter-American Affairs in the 1940s, Nelson dispatched Lockwood on a fact-finding tour of Latin America. When Nelson became assistant secretary of state, Lockwood moved with him. After the war, Lockwood shunned Milbank and joined Curtis, Mallet-Prevost, Colt & Mosle, which had an international-trade practice.

When Lockwood was tapped to replace Debevoise, opinion within the Rockefeller empire was divided about whether he should return to Milbank or perhaps join another firm. Winthrop Aldrich, John McCloy, and Morris Hadley, a Milbank name partner, met to discuss Lockwood's fate, Lockwood recalled from his tiny retirement quarters in Milbank's uptown offices. Partly on the basis of his own recommendation, they decided he should rejoin Milbank.

"When I came to be Mr. Rockefeller Jr.'s lawyer," he said, "I left Curtis, Mallet. I just realized that all of the history of the Rockefellers was in Milbank, this firm. If I was going to be his lawyer, I couldn't really do it from Curtis, Mallet. . . . I felt Milbank had all the records, all the background, had worked on the accumulation of property."

Lockwood acted as liaison between Milbank and the family for twenty years, and during that time his firm rarely had to worry about the future of the relationship. Milbank's special connection with the Rockefellers was further protected by Lockwood's peculiar setup. He became only a part-time partner at the firm, spending most of his time in Room 5600, the family's suite of offices at Rockefeller Center. His compensation was provided in roughly equal halves by the firm and the family.

Lockwood recruited Milbank associates to do approximately two-year stints in the family office. In 1963 Squire N. Bozorth, then a trusts and estates associate, moved uptown. He eventually returned to Milbank and became a partner, overseeing the trusts and estates needs of family members. "The Rockefeller legal office became more and more institutionalized, if you will, with a footing of [its] own," said Bozorth. "With the passage of time all of the lawyers came to be employees of the family."

As a matter of course, Room 5600 had about three in-house lawyers. But they were usually Milbank alumni and their boss was Lockwood. Throughout the Lockwood period, he and Milbank were intimately involved in the Rockefellers' favorite projects. It was Lockwood who drafted a 1946 letter from Junior to the United Nations about a possible donation, and discussed it with him over breakfast. Junior's $8.5 million check, one of the few checks he ever wrote, paid for the East Side Manhattan plot of land on which the UN was built. A photograph of the check was framed on Lockwood's wall in his Milbank retirement office.

Milbank was also attendant at the birth of another Rockefeller-family project in the late 1950s and early 1960s: Lincoln Center for the Performing Arts. Junior's son, John D. Rockefeller III, was deeply committed to building an arts center on the West Side of Manhattan. He raised money for its development and became its chairman. The firm oversaw even the smallest legal details of the project. Larry Nelson, who later became head of Milbank's real estate group, obtained a liquor license for Lincoln Center. Peter Herman laughingly called himself an expert on the Lincoln Center garage.

Lockwood planned to retire when he was sixty-five, in 1969. His impending departure precipitated a discussion about who should do the family's legal work. Not all the Cousins were comfortable with the handling of their legacy by Room 5600, Collier and Horowitz reported in *The Rockefellers*. According to Lockwood, that unease extended to the handling of the family's legal affairs. "Young Rockefellers thought we ought to go to any law firm we wanted," Lockwood recalled, adding that it never became a serious issue. "They wondered why they shouldn't go to their own lawyers." The Cousins also questioned whether it wasn't cheaper to use in-house lawyers instead of Milbank, which for the most part was paid at its regular hourly rates.

Lockwood explained to them that estate and tax planning should be done by one set of lawyers. It was true, after all, that only lawyers at Milbank had intimate knowledge of the network of trusts that held the Rockefeller fortune. Partner Carroll L. Wainwright, Jr., himself a descendant of robber baron Jay Gould, was counsel to the committee in charge of the giant 1934 trusts set up by Junior to transfer his wealth to his sons. Wainwright had replaced a deceased Milbank partner. Milbank lawyers had drafted the five powerful Brothers' (and their sister's) wills and had administered the estates of John D. Rockefeller, Sr., his son, and the deceased members of the Brothers generation. And so Lockwood told the Cousins that it was probably cheaper to use Milbank, which knew the family's work inside out.

Several Milbank partners, including older members of the firm, were considered as possible replacements for Lockwood. Donal O'Brien, a young trusts-and-estates partner who had done a stint in Room 5600 under Lockwood's tutelage, was finally selected. "He was very attractive to the [family members] who liked big open spaces—the conservationists—Winthrop and Nelson," Lockwood recalled almost twenty years into his retirement. Several members of the Brothers generation, Lockwood said, "thought he was right for their sons. . . . He was a thinking person and interested in all sorts of things."

Like Lockwood, O'Brien had divided loyalties. In

his capacity as counsel to "the uptown client," as the Rockefellers were called by Milbank lawyers after the family office was moved from the Standard Oil Building in lower Manhattan to 30 Rockefeller Plaza, he was a member of the firm committee. In Room 5600, he was a key staffer paid in part by the family. The arrangement was awkward, especially in an increasingly large operation that functioned more like a corporation than a family office.

And so in 1983, under pressure from the family, O'Brien relinquished his Milbank partnership and became a full-time employee of the Rockefellers.* Lawyers at Milbank said O'Brien withdrew from the firm—and of course from the firm committee—at the request of his client.

"We decided he was doing so much here that it really didn't make sense for him to be a partner there," said David Rockefeller. At that time, he said, the family was trying to get its office under one roof. The family thought "we shouldn't feel bound to use Milbank regardless," said Rockefeller. He says he and others at 5600 believed O'Brien's departure from Milbank would give him "a greater sense of freedom" and "a bit more independence" from Milbank. O'Brien declined to discuss his relationship with his client. Bozorth, his former

*In an interview in 1990, David Rockefeller said that as part of an effort to reorganize the family office, he and others were revisiting the 1983 decision to bring O'Brien in-house. He said they were considering trying to affiliate the family's in-house lawyers with an outside firm. A Rockefeller family staffer said that firm would likely be Milbank, but that the conversations were so preliminary that the idea had not yet been broached with the firm.

trusts and estates partner, said he thought it "just got complicated for O'Brien to be both an employee of the family and a member of the firm." There were "people in the family who wanted their counsel to be wholly their own," he said. Real estate partner Peter Herman added that Room 5600 wanted any appearance of conflict removed.

Suddenly Milbank's most solid client relationship was less secure. The family had over the years occasionally used other firms, including Patterson, Belknap; Debevoise & Plimpton and Willkie Farr & Gallagher, the new firm of Bruce M. Montgomerie, who in 1983 became the first Milbank partner ever to defect to another law firm. But they were no longer the firm's chief competitors for the family's personal work. Instead, Milbank's rival now was the administrative and legal staffs of its own client.

Milbank was still widely known as the Rockefellers' law firm. It continued to attract other illustrious clients, such as members of the Johnson and Getty families, based on that reputation. But the trusts and estates partners, who once had even taken care of the Rockefellers' traffic tickets, found themselves gradually distanced from their favorite family. Milbank still drafted Rockefeller will and trust documents, but often O'Brien's Room 5600 team would meet first with the family member and simply convey his or her desires to the lawyers at Milbank with many of the options already decided. In the past, Bozorth and O'Brien had met with family members together to discuss their trusts and estates needs. Bozorth, in fact, still occasionally dealt face-to-face with the remaining members of the Brothers generation, David and Laurance. One reason for the lessened direct contact between Milbank and the Rockefellers, Bozorth felt, was the growth in the size of the family. The twenty-two Cousins had roughly fifty-four children. "With a twenty-one-year-old member of the family, it doesn't make sense to gear up a middle-aged partner at Milbank, Tweed to go up and meet with them," said Bozorth. "The extent of my direct dealings with members of the Fifth Generation are pretty limited."

Peter Herman liked to joke that he could get into the Rockefeller-family office without triggering alarms. When he passed through Room 5600's doors, however, it was almost inevitably not to see a family member, but a member of the professional staff. Herman represented David Rockefeller and other family members in real estate deals. He handled the sale of the L'Enfant Plaza in Washington and the development of the Embarcadero Center in San Francisco. He talked to David's chief of staff often, but only rarely dealt with his client face to face.

Donald B. Brant, Jr., a member of the Oresman group, represented Rockefeller & Co. Inc., the family's investment-advisory arm. He was also counsel to family members who were shareholders in International Basic Economy Corporation, a Latin American development company set up by Nelson Rockefeller as a profit-making enterprise. Like Bozorth, he found himself increasingly dealing with in-house lawyers, especially David Strawbridge, an ex-Milbank associate who worked on O'Brien's staff. "Back thirty years ago, when the family office was really controlled by the senior family members, there would have been more direct contact," said Brant in 1987. "I think this relationship is becoming more institutionalized and it's natural that it would." Brant, a securities lawyer, had met with family members only on three or four occasions in the previous eight years, when individual family members were interested in setting up or financing a business.

In the mid-1980s, the kinds of work Milbank did for the Rockefellers also changed. There were no major deaths in the family to keep members of the trusts and estates department busy. Milbank had been involved in about a dozen of the family's real estate projects between 1976 and 1983, but the family then reduced its real estate development business and sold some properties off. Herman found himself devoting a greater portion of his time to a nascent computer practice.

David Rockefeller said that one reason less of the family's personal work was done with Milbank was that many younger members of the family had connections with other law firms. "I don't think it's because of any dissatisfaction with Milbank," he said. He said fewer members of the family used Chase as their bank. "There isn't the same sense of identity with either the bank or the firm that there was when there were fewer family members," he said. He called the change in attitude "inevitable."

More and more, RGI was the focal point of Milbank's Rockefeller business. RGI, once called Rockefeller Center Inc., was mostly owned by family trusts. Its primary asset was Rockefeller Center, yet it had branched into communications as well. As RGI diversified, acquiring and disposing of companies, more work was created for Al Lilley, the member of the firm committee who oversaw the company's corporate work. "Lilley played a supporting role to us five or eight years ago," Herman said. "Now we are in a supporting relationship to Lilley."

Bozorth put it this way: "All the little bunnies from under the basket—they run out from time to time and sometimes they move around under the basket."

Only five months after the purchase of the land, Lilley and a large Milbank team became heavily embroiled in one of the family's most publicized deals ever: the mortgaging of Rockefeller Center. The $1.3 billion financing was the largest in real estate history. The deal was a plum assignment for Milbank, a sign that the relationship was intact and thriving. After all, nine partners and eleven associates from the Lilley group and the real estate and tax departments put in long hours on the financing. They worked for five months alongside Sullivan & Cromwell, counsel to Goldman, Sachs & Co., the lead underwriter for the financing. For Milbank, it was good news that when the Rockefellers had a big-league task they still turned to the same law firm that had once handled their parking tickets.

It was precisely the kind of matter an in-house lawyer would hire an outside law firm to handle. Liquefying a real estate asset—even almost twelve acres in midtown Manhattan—is not difficult. The family could have simply sold the land and the buildings on it. That transaction would not have been appreciably more complicated than the Columbia land purchase Green had overseen earlier in the year. But the Rockefellers—especially senior members of the family—did not want to give up ownership of the property. "For both emotional and financial reasons they didn't want to sell it," said Robert M. Thomas, Jr., the Sullivan & Cromwell partner who represented Goldman, Sachs. "It's something that's been associated with the family since it was built. It's got their name on it."

Also, a huge tax assessment would have been levied on the family if they had sold the property outright. New York's steep tax on real estate gains meant that the Rockefellers might have had to fork over up to $200 million in taxes—half the price they had paid Columbia for the land.

Those two constraints on the financing created obstacles for the lawyers involved in the deal. In order to minimize taxes and maximize the family's access to cash, the deal was structured as a real estate investment trust, commonly known as a REIT. A company structured as a REIT pays no taxes so long as it meets certain conditions set forth by the IRS. The plan was for the REIT to issue $1.3 billion in securities. It would then make a loan to RGI, which presumably would make the cash available to family members in one way or another. The REIT issued three kinds of securities: $750 million in common stock, $335 million in current-coupon convertible debentures, and $215 million in zero-coupon convertible debentures.

For investors, the stock and debt had several attractions. The most obvious was that by buying the securities the investor had a piece of one of the most glamorous properties in the world. In a sense they became partners with the Rockefellers. A far more significant selling point was the equity kicker built into the deal by Milbank; Sullivan & Cromwell; and Goldman, Sachs. Rockefeller Center Properties, the REIT created by Milbank, had the option on December 31, 2000, to convert its $1.3 billion loan to the family into a 71.5-percent stake in the partnership that owned the buildings, skating rink, and land that was Rockefeller Center.

The complexity of the deal required the full intellectual muscle of the Milbank team. It was the kind of deal that any corporate law firm would be proud of. But this deal was not Milbank's alone. When problems arose, as they do in any such transaction, it was Green who weighed the interests of his clients versus the marketability of the securities. And it was Green who acted as chief liaison between the lawyers and the corporate staff at RGI. According to Lilley, there was no real hierarchy among the lawyers—"except that Jonathan Green was the boss."

The deal closed in late 1985 and was deemed a success, although there were some press reports that the stock had been priced too high and that investors had been induced to buy in because of the allure of the Rockefeller name. The Rockefellers were roughly $1.3

billion richer. Some of that money went to pay off loans for the Columbia land, but a big chunk of what remained was put into the 1934 trusts which held much of the family's wealth. It was a controversial move. In removing the cash from RGI, the family was taking the money out of the business so that it could be used to further their own personal interests.

"The essence of the deal was to extract the value of that bundle of assets, that real estate up there," said Lilley from his downtown Manhattan office. There was, Lilley explained delicately, "a desire for some time to diversify that investment, or provide liquidity of that investment. There has been some pressure for a period of time . . . to make distributions." *Fortune* magazine labeled the young Rockefellers who were clamoring for liquidity the "cash-out generations," and mourned the passing of the dominance of the Rockefellers in the business world.

And so, though the deal had been heralded as good news by the Milbank lawyers who worked on it, the many billable hours had masked a shocking truth: In the future Milbank might not do many more significant deals for the Rockefellers simply because the Rockefellers might not be doing them.* The young Rockefellers who had gained from the transaction included doctors, teach-

*In 1990, Mitsubishi Estates, a giant Japanese real estate developer, acquired a 51-percent stake in RGI. Milbank represented the Rockefeller family in the deal. Green said that RGI would probably use Dewey, Ballantine, which represented Mitsubishi Estates, from time to time. "There will be lots of firms that represent us," Green said, "and Milbank will be one of them."

ers, and a U.S. senator. Nelson's son Rodman, an active real estate investor and an important client of Milbank's real estate department, was an exception. Still, it was hard to imagine a new Rockefeller Center or Lincoln Center for the Milbank lawyers to work on in the fore-seeable future.

David Rockefeller said that his relatives had fewer legal needs than in past years. "They're younger and have less money," he said. And even if a large Rocke-feller family project did materialize, it was becoming more and more obvious that Milbank's role would no longer be a certainty. In 1986, RGI hired Shearman & Sterling to handle two major Manhattan real estate deals. In the first, RGI bought Time Inc.'s 45-percent interest in the Time & Life building at Rockefeller Center for $118 million. RGI owned the remaining 55 per-cent of the building. In the other 1986 deal, Exxon Corporation and RGI sold the Exxon Building, which they owned jointly, to Mitsui Fudosan (New York) Inc. for $610 million.

Green said RGI decided to use Lee A. Kuntz of Shearman & Sterling because Stevan Sandberg, the in-house lawyer shepherding the deals, had once worked at Shearman & Sterling. "He just felt comfortable using Lee Kuntz and his team to do the two transactions," explained Green. "I said, 'Fine.'"

Milbank took note of their exclusion from the two deals; Green recalled getting a call from a Milbank part-ner asking why they hadn't gotten the work.

Green experimented with other firms as well. He

asked Paul, Weiss to help RGI put together investment-fund vehicles. Hiring the firm was "a matter of getting somebody else's viewpoint. [There was] no particular reason. They have a good reputation." Among the other firms he used were Proskauer Rosen Goetz & Mendelsohn; Paul, Hastings, Janofsky & Walker, a Los Angeles firm; and Bachner Tally Polevoy & Misher, a New York firm that helped RGI with tenant problems at Rockefeller Center.

It was clear that Milbank would have to learn to compete with other law firms as their relationship with their oldest client evolved. The Rockefellers had become a client like any other. The intimacy between Milbank and the family was gone. Ancient partners recalled close ties, even friendships, with their Rockefeller clients. Lockwood remembered sharing meals with Junior and his wife. Rice Brewster recounted being transfixed by an Andrew Wyeth painting while waiting to enter the office of one of the Rockefeller Brothers.

Those were memories of a sort that the next generation of Milbank lawyers would never have.

5

MILBANK'S
BANKING
EDUCATION

IN THE MID-1980S, MIL-
bank was also learning to adjust to its uneasy relationship
with Chase. Not since the merger of Chase Bank and
the Manhattan National Bank in the 1950s had Milbank's relationship with Chase been so vulnerable.

From the late 1970s through much of the 1980s,
there was persistent tension between the two institutions.
The bank was trying to shed its conservative image in
an increasingly competitive marketplace. But Milbank
had trouble making the transition with the bank. Gen-

erations of partners had been trained to give risk-adverse advice. As the bank modernized, Milbank was caught between two eras. And because the partners were often unable to grasp the bankers' legal needs, Milbank lost out on some important Chase business.

In 1986, however, it was still possible to ignore the truth about the Chase relationship. Milbank was deeply involved in a longstanding and frustrating Chase crisis—the renegotiation of Third World debt that had plagued many of the United States' big banks. The crisis stemmed from practices of the 1960s and 1970s, when large banks, flush with deposits from oil companies and oil-rich nations, shoveled billions of dollars at developing nations, especially in Latin America. All was fine until the late 1970s, when these nations started missing their giant interest payments.

Milbank was appointed counsel to committees formed to represent the banks that had lent money to Venezuela and Ecuador. Chase was co-chairman of both committees. The renegotiation of Venezuela's public-sector debt—over $25 billion—was arduous and complex. Logan, partner Peter D. Rowntree, and three associates spent hours hammering out Venezuela's economic fate in Conference Room 48D—dubbed the Venezuela Room—on the forty-eighth floor of Chase Manhattan Plaza. On February 24, 1986, after a succession of roadblocks, representatives from the approximately 400 banks that had lent Venezuela money signed thirteen restructuring agreements in Chase's huge auditorium on the first floor of its office tower.

The Milbank lawyers knew that the agreement would likely have to be negotiated again. Frustrating and tedious as the talks were, however, it was lucrative work. Although the years of Venezuela negotiations were good for Milbank's bottom line, the many billable hours clouded the vision of those partners who didn't want to see the truth about Chase: the bank still called on Milbank for crisis work, but there were cracks in the relationship.

Milbank's problems adapting to the changes at Chase could be traced to the ghost of Roy Haberkern, who had taught an entire generation of partners how to think about the bank's business. Toward the end of his career, it had become obvious that Haberkern's approach to advising the bank was inflexible and outmoded. The strains in the relationship had begun to show up shortly before he left and escalated over the next decade.

Haberkern's dedication to Chase had been legendary even outside the firm. When it came to the welfare of Chase Manhattan, not even the smallest detail had escaped Haberkern's attention. At a meeting with David Rockefeller, Haberkern had even expressed concern that bird droppings would mar *Group of Four Trees,* a huge black-and-white painted sculpture of Jean Dubuffet installed at Chase Manhattan Plaza in 1972.

"He knew the bank so well that he had a good sense for how senior management of the bank would react to something," said Chase general counsel Edward Shaw, a one-time Milbank partner. Haberkern had had the trust of David Rockefeller, and when it came to legal questions, partners at Milbank and officers at Chase followed his lead without question. A former Chase in-house lawyer recalled being told by fellow Chase staffers, " 'We always do it this way because Roy told us to.' No one knew the reason. There were no memos."

In the late 1970s, Haberkern's world changed dramatically. The bank's gigantic loans to the Third World and the energy industry turned out to be bad risks, and for the first time in most bankers' and banking lawyers' memories, consumer banking became an important profit center. Chase also struggled to keep up with Citibank, which was testing the regulatory constraints on interstate banking and investment banking by commercial banks. David Rockefeller and Roy Haberkern were conservatives, and in every way they epitomized the old banking attitudes. Haberkern was risk-adverse. He had no taste for the new, cutting-edge banking businesses— those that came dangerously close to the regulatory limits. If something was "legally feasible but risky, he would tell his partner that was a dumb thing to recommend," said a Chase staffer. A former Citibank vice president who admired Haberkern added, "Roy Haberkern worked very hard to keep the world from changing."

As David Rockefeller neared retirement, he and his bankers realized that they had to make concessions to the new climate Citibank was shepherding in. Chase took up the challenge, albeit with great caution. In 1976 Rockefeller brought in Robert Douglass as executive vice president and general counsel. Douglass had dedicated much of his career to the Rockefeller family, serving as a top aide to Nelson Rockefeller. Though Douglass joined Al Lilley's group at Milbank when Rockefeller became Gerald Ford's vice president in 1974, he never became imbued with Milbank's culture.

Douglass had two mandates at Chase, both of which had a profound effect on Milbank. One was to revitalize the bank's legal department. Fees were skyrocketing and most large corporations were learning that it was more cost-effective to do routine work in-house. His other role, more significant, was to help the bank find a way to compete in the new banking environment. Douglass was an outside man, and he provided senior management with a different perspective, a renewed confidence to find their way. "Douglass advocated change and the institution wanted to change, but they felt more comfortable having Douglass tell them how," said a former Chase officer. "He guided Chase in terms of what does Chase want to look like."

Nominally, Douglass had replaced an older lawyer, Louis A. Russo, who had retired. Russo had not been a significant player in the higher reaches of the corporation; the senior bankers had seen Haberkern as their lawyer. Russo's department had practiced a brand of law that was unsophisticated and unambitious. His small group of lawyers had spent much of their time handling small real estate loans and answering questions from branches, typically about bounced checks. Their work had negligible impact on a bank making multimillion-dollar loans to Third World nations and large companies, selling participations in those loans to other banks, and testing the regulatory waters for the first time.

In essence, Douglass had taken Haberkern's job. Although Haberkern later called the decision to expand the legal department "wise," at the time it must have given the aging Milbank partner a jolt, because the territory had been solely his for as long as most of his partners could remember. With the advent of Douglass's stewardship, the role of the in-house department at Chase would never be the same. Henceforth the chief inside lawyer—not the outside lawyer—would call the shots.

The unexpected announcement that he would retire in 1979 perhaps shouldn't have been so surprising to Haberkern's partners. The needs of the bank and the firm had changed so suddenly that he may have felt he had no choice. In an interview long after he retired, Haberkern said that he had "worked my tail off all my life" and was planning to retire but had not yet decided when. At a meeting of Chase officers at a resort owned by Laurance Rockefeller, Haberkern and David Rockefeller took a walk around the block "a couple of times," Haberkern recalled. They decided it "wasn't a good idea for both of us to go out at the same time." And so it was decided that Haberkern would retire a year before his client.

David Rockefeller called Haberkern a "good friend" and an "extraordinarily able man, but he was also a very strong personality and I think tended not to want to see Chase have a strong legal department because he liked to manage the whole thing himself." Haberkern, he said, "rather overshadowed other people. That isn't a criticism but it means here was someone outside the bank playing more of a role than I think was appropriate."

It fell to Logan to keep the relationship intact. He took over the Chase account and chairmanship of Milbank's banking department when Haberkern retired. Logan, then forty-eight, was Haberkern's natural successor. He had started his career as a corporate associate in Roger Oresman's group. In 1959, when he was a fourth-year associate, Logan had been spirited away by Haberkern to become the fourth lawyer in the banking department. Haberkern, still trying to keep Dewey, Ballantine at a safe distance from his precious client, had needed fresh talent, and Logan had already developed a reputation as one of the brightest men in the firm.

Logan's manner was severe. Somehow the timeless business suits most Milbankers wore looked even more conservative on him. He wore heavy black glasses and always appeared to be tense. His speech was precise and his voice almost prissy.

He was hard to get to know. He was born in Evanston, Illinois, and his family had roots in Montana. On the wall of his airy but nondescript corner office hung correspondence between Lincoln and Logan's great-great-grandfather, an Illinois newspaper publisher. The down-home expressions he occasionally used during Venezuela debt negotiations surprised others in the room. Like the rest of his partners, Logan had all the badges of wealth: a Fifth Avenue apartment, a country home in Redding Ridge, Connecticut, and an entry in the Social Register. But he hid his ambition and assertiveness behind a mask of self-deprecation that seemed increasingly out of place as the legal market became more competitive. He called himself "just another working stiff," and described his appointment as Haberkern's successor as "a notable lapse in the firm's good judgment."

In some respects Logan was similar to Haberkern. He, too, devoted his life to serving "the Chase," as he reverently put it. Like his predecessor, he put in brutal hours and became known as one of the nation's most knowledgeable banking lawyers. But conservative and cautious as he was, Logan saw that there was a new awkwardness between the firm and its longtime client. He also knew that resistance to the newcomers downstairs could ultimately spell disaster for the firm. If Chase was going to change, Logan decided, the best way to maintain the relationship was for Milbank to change along with it.

The period after Logan took Haberkern's place was a difficult one for Milbank's banking lawyers. They had to adjust not only to new, complex banking products and a dramatic increase in the size of financings, but also to the bankers' changing views of the role of lawyers and their impatience with the conservatism drummed into a generation of Milbank lawyers by Haberkern.

Milbank's banking lawyers, of course, did not have a corner on conservatism in law firms. Entrepreneurial executives often complain about overly cautious lawyers.

At Citibank, in the early 1980s, a young aggressive executive named John S. Reed was growing impatient with Shearman & Sterling, which he considered too mired in tradition. He began to turn to other firms he considered to be more aggressive, including Weil, Gotshal & Manges. In the banking community, Milbank was perceived as even more conservative than Shearman & Sterling.

Writer Charles R. Morris, a former Chase vice president, recalled trying to develop a new product to offer a huge oil company, which entailed securing loans with gasoline receivables. The "securitization" of assets is now commonplace, but in the early 1980s, when Morris worked at Chase, it was new. The trick for Chase bankers was to get innovative financing past John A. Hooper, who was in charge of credit policy at Chase. Morris, who had been assistant New York City budget director during Mayor John Lindsay's administration, remembered being cautioned about Milbank by a more experienced Chase hand. He was warned not to reveal the project to the credit manager prematurely and to be coy with Milbank. "The line to Milbank was very close. They were inclined to call Hooper . . . if they thought it was risky," Morris said he was told.

During his first years with the bank, Douglass stocked the legal department with bright lights, some capable of tackling the kind of work Milbank did. He brought in young talent from Shearman & Sterling; Cravath, Swaine & Moore; Rogers & Wells; and Weil, Gotshal & Manges—firms that Milbank competed with for law-school graduates. Sorting out just who was making assignments—Chase's bankers or its lawyers—was ticklish. Milbank had contracts with hundreds of Chase bankers who typically called on the firm when they put a loan together. Douglass had to sell his in-house lawyers to the bankers. Some Chase bankers were fed up with Milbank, but the majority were comfortable with their longtime counselors. They thought of in-house lawyers as unsophisticated, not up to the caliber of work done by Milbank. Sometimes they would call the firm and the in-house department for advice, and choose which verdict they liked better.

One young lawyer Douglass recruited from a top firm remembered an interrogation by a bank officer who "interviewed me like I was a first-year law student . . . and proceeded to tell me what he thought of the in-house department and told me he wanted to have Milbank review my work. I said I didn't work that way."

If anyone was up to the job of convincing bankers to use in-house lawyers it was Douglass. Though he had practiced law only sporadically, he had acquired impressive political skills while serving as Nelson Rockefeller's aide. Douglass acted as liaison between the bankers and his fledgling group of in-house lawyers. "When we wanted to bring work in-house, he had no problem with it, and no problem telling departments we were doing the work in-house," said the former Chase lawyer from the early days of the rejuvenated legal department. "He in his way sold the institution on using us, on giving us a chance, by not shoving us down their throats. I think he leveraged off his successes. I think he had this ability to pick his battles. . . . Eventually he got almost everything he wanted." Douglass was a glad-hander. He had a keen mind and quickly won people over. "He could charm the skin off a snake," said Elliot Ganz, who worked in the Chase legal department for three years.

The reaction of Milbank's banking partners to the lawyers on Chase's payroll varied. "There was a good deal of tension as we were building up the department," said Robert B. Adams, the only holdover from the old legal department to play a key managerial role during Douglass's regime. "After Bob [Douglass] came, there was quite a bit of tension and there was not a close working relationship between Milbank and the legal de-partment despite [the fact] that he came from Milbank."

The growth of the in-house department, Logan said deliberately in the mid-1980s when Chase had fifty-five in-house lawyers, was "very certainly a basis for concern, but not a basis for resentment."

"It's not just a question of a bigger staff. But these guys are really very good," Logan said two years later when the in-house legal staff had grown to about seventy lawyers. "It's important for us to develop a supportive and complementary relationship with these staffs. It's a daily challenge, not only personal relationships as you can imagine, but [in] not reinventing the wheel. . . . It's really important to develop a positive view about this fact of life."

The in-house lawyer who joined up soon after

Douglass's arrival described Logan as "accessible," a kudo from a young professional fighting for acceptance from Chase officers and the Milbank lawyers upstairs. Partner Edward Shaw, one of the banking department's shining young lights, also earned a reputation for his hospitable attitude toward the bank's in-house lawyers. But not all of Logan's partners were so enlightened. Turf battles developed between Chase and Milbank lawyers over deals and even documents. Sometimes the Milbankers tried to ignore the in-house lawyers they supposedly worked for. They would conveniently forget to send them copies of memos or keep them abreast of developments on deals.

One of the Milbank partners whom the in-house lawyers found infuriating was Frank Puleo, who, like Shaw, was a rising banking star. Puleo's name was often paired with Worenklein's even though Puleo was several years older and the two young partners had distinctly different personal styles. Both were bright, aggressive, and envisioned a new luster for Milbank. They were management maniacs, and lobbied for "growth and diversification." In a sense they competed for the privilege of being the youngest member of Milbank's management team. But Puleo steered a more moderate course.

Puleo was extremely cool. He rarely confided the secrets of the partnership even to associates who worked closely with him. His calls for a more modern outlook on the legal marketplace were tamer than Worenklein's exhortations. Puleo encouraged his partners to "get out into the traffic." The message was the same as Worenklein's, but the implication—that if one was in the mainstream of business it would somehow bump into you—was more palatable to those partners who thought that Worenklein's approach came perilously close to an unethical call to solicit business.

Puleo was increasingly important to Chase. He was smart and capable of looking at big-picture issues, especially regulatory matters involving the expansion of the limits of commercial banking. But as the legal department expanded, Puleo developed a reputation for being "obstructionist and getting in the way of things getting done," according to Ganz, the former Chase lawyer.

Some in-house lawyers found him patronizing. "I found working with Frank Puleo very difficult. He had a high-and-mighty kind of attitude," said the lawyer recruited by Douglass early in his tenure with Chase. "He was one of the people who would bypass you, and you were always in the position of having to call him and catch up. We were not as clever, we were not as smart. He was just one of those people I wouldn't want on my team, even though he was very good."

Puleo said he did not intend to be obstructionist—although, he added, "I may have been a little slow. . . . Certainly as the department gained in its own capabilities I became more aware of it. As I became more aware of it I tried to be constructive and supportive."

The most overt skirmish between Milbank and the legal department came over the development of Chase's consumer businesses. Like other huge banks, Chase had

MILBANK'S BANKING EDUCATION

traditionally made its profits from commercial and international loans. Senior bankers looked down on the revolution in consumer banking—the growth of credit-card businesses and new consumer lending products. They didn't see it as a prestige area.

Chase, as usual, was playing catch-up with Citicorp in consumer banking. John Reed had convinced South Dakota that if it changed its usury laws—and allowed financial institutions to charge higher interest rates—he would move some of Citicorp's credit-card business to the state. South Dakota's legislature and governor, eager for the thousands of jobs Citicorp would provide, gladly obliged.

The timing of Chase's decision to target consumer banking as an area of growth roughly coincided with Douglass's push to upgrade the legal staff. Consumer banking was the perfect ground on which to test the efficacy of the legal department. Milbank, like many of Chase's senior bankers, hadn't shown great interest in the field. Significantly, one of the key bank officers who spearheaded the growth of the consumer area had no allegiance to Milbank. He was Frederick Hammer, an entrepreneurial executive who had worked at Bankers Trust. Hammer's hiring in 1977 was unusual because Chase, like its law firm, eschewed lateral hiring on a senior level; most of its top-level officers were home-grown. Hammer's marketing background was another departure for the bank. He had been director of research at the Federal Deposit Insurance Corporation (FDIC) and a vice president at Associates Corporation of North America, a finance and insurance company.

Douglass and Hammer worked well together. One of their first big projects was the startup of the bank's credit-card and consumer unit. It was a complicated business. Running the credit-card operation out of One Chase Manhattan Plaza was not an option. Usury laws in New York were too stringent. Chase considered South Dakota, Rhode Island, and Delaware as possible sites for its operation. Delaware Governor Pierre S. du Pont was more than willing to make regulatory concessions to a potentially giant employer. The governor and his aides negotiated with Chase president and chief operating officer Thomas G. Labrecque, Douglass, and Hammer, and Chase Delaware USA was born.

Milbank helped draft a new consumer-credit code for the state, but on most aspects of the deal the Chase team relied on the in-house staff. The work involved lobbying and the preparation of a banking application. The bank's management closely watched the in-house lawyers' performance—and apparently they were pleased.

Throughout most of the 1970s, none of Milbank's banking partners had specialized in consumer work. They looked down on the field as unsophisticated and unworthy of their talent. Whatever consumer work there was tended to flow to Jeffrey S. Tallackson, an associate.

In late 1978, Tallackson had come up for partner. He was bright but wasn't a favorite of the banking partners. In most cases, a young lawyer with expertise in an area outside the mainstream of his department's work wouldn't have had a chance of making partner. But Tallackson had come of age just as it became clear that Chase was eager to dive into the consumer-banking craze. Haberkern had become his big backer. He said he felt "absolute loyalty" to Tallackson for having taken on the consumer work and done a "very, very great job." As usual, Haberkern had put the relationship between Milbank and Chase ahead of everything else. According to a tale that became well known in some Milbank circles, some of the banking partners had been reluctant to elevate Tallackson, but Haberkern had argued that someone had to look after the bank's consumer needs. "Are *you* going to do consumer banking work?" Haberkern had asked his partners, according to an associate of that time. "Then you'd better make Jeffrey Tallackson a partner." They did. He became a partner on January 1, 1979.

During the next few years it became painfully obvious that Hammer and Tallackson were not a great combination. Hammer was brash. He was a marketer. His audience was the plain folk he hoped would gobble up Chase's consumer products. Tallackson, good-humored as he was, had been trained at Milbank. His work was careful and complete. He left no stone unturned. And that translated into tremendous legal bills. When Tallackson drafted credit-card or revolving-credit agreements, the results were tedious, long, and protective of the bank. Hammer wanted a more consumer-oriented—or consumer-friendly—approach.

Hammer didn't abandon Milbank immediately. In 1983, he asked the firm to help negotiate the purchase of Rose & Co. Investment Brokers Inc., a discount brokerage. He heavily relied on Sidley & Austin, a huge Chicago-based firm, and Chase's in-house lawyers as well. But he soon decided he didn't want Milbank lawyers on his team. The Milbankers made him impatient because they were too cautious, too slow, and answered his questions with long reports. Hammer was very budget-conscious, and he didn't want to pay for long memos. He wanted quick, efficient advice.

In the early 1980s, Hammer got a plan accepted by Chase's top management to expand the bank's consumer financial services—a panoply of loans, certificates of deposit, and credit-card services—across the country. He asked Tallackson to survey the law in various states in which he was interested in doing business. Tallackson's report provided endless detail on the applicable law in each state. "They were fabulous pieces, but they went on forever," said a former Chase staffer.

Tallackson had fallen into the trap that often trips up conservative lawyers who work for innovative executives. He had spent too many words telling Hammer what he couldn't pursue legally. Hammer said he decided that he couldn't "afford these great big studies. . . . The problem, it seems to me, is if you're in a law firm dealing with a client, you write something down—you have to be sure you're right. You have to have all the footnotes. [I want to know] can I do it? . . . I don't really want to know how to do it. I'll worry about dotting the *i*'s and crossing the *t*'s later."

Tallackson's survey was the last substantial piece of work he did for Hammer. "That particular study probably convinced us we should do all of this in-house," said Hammer, who nevertheless called Tallackson "outstanding—a terrific lawyer." He felt he was paying huge bills for routine legal work. He got the impression that Milbank wasn't giving Tallackson the support he needed. The turnaround time was disappointing. "It became clear that this was a whole body of law just evolving. Since everyone was learning, why pay the tuition cost of the outside lawyers?" asked Hammer, who later became chairman of Meritor Financial Group, a Philadelphia-based bank holding company. "We started to do more and more in-house, and we didn't do much outside."

The young in-house lawyers who became members of Hammer's team adapted his style. Their written answers to his queries were to the point and not laden with legalese. They were knowledgeable about federal regulations and consumer-finance laws. If they needed assistance they turned to local counsel who knew their states' laws. In 1981 and 1982 the in-housers helped Chase start finance companies in Florida, California, Arizona, Colorado, and Utah. In 1983, Douglass hired a young lawyer from the Federal Reserve, Robert C. Plows, who was capable of handling Chase's consumer-credit work. "After that point, I don't believe I had another conversation with Milbank, Tweed," said Hammer.

Milbank's exclusion from a growing practice area was an expensive loss for the firm. In the first phase of Chase's expansion, the bank opened twenty-seven personal financial services offices in eighteen states. By the end of 1987, there were fifty-three such offices in twenty-one states. Chase Delaware USA had become a $5.9 billion business.

Milbank's partners felt that the problems had not escalated into an emergency, and they had good reason to feel that way. Like other large corporations, Chase had learned that while it was cost effective to take some work in-house, outside firms were ideal in a crisis. Big firms could throw an unlimited number of troops at a problem, and they were more likely to have skills needed only rarely by a client.

In 1982, two scandals exploded that increased Milbank's bottom line. In May, Drysdale Government Securities Inc., a new player in the securities market, went under. Chase had lent securities it was holding for other banks and brokers to Drysdale, which in turn had used them as short-term collateral in other transactions. When Drysdale failed, it owed Chase $285 million in interest that the bank was supposed to pass on to the banks and brokers for which it held the bonds.

The bank was still reeling from the loss and the resulting bad press when Penn Square Bank was shut down by the Comptroller of the Currency in July. The Oklahoma City–based bank, headquartered in a small office in a shopping center, had syndicated $2 billion in oil and gas loans. Chase and other banks had purchased loans of dubious value from the high-flying Oklahoma bank. Chase carried $212 million of the shaky, poorly documented loans on its books.

Two teams of Milbank lawyers were pressed into emergency service. There was no question about whether in-house or outside lawyers would ford through the reams of documents involved. These shows were to be Milbank productions. Eight litigation lawyers toiled on Drysdale nearly full-time for over two years. The Penn Square debacle kept a small herd of Milbank lawyers, mostly from John Jerome's bankruptcy group, billing extraordinary hours. But the two crises didn't completely distract Chase from its national banking strategy. And even as Milbank lawyers toiled on Drysdale and Penn Square, in-house lawyers were assuming more legal power within Chase. Douglass had found his place in the upper echelons of Chase's management. He had taken charge of the bank's strategic-planning and corporate-communications staffs.

By 1983 it was time to bring in a new general counsel so that Douglass could move on. An obvious candidate was Bob Adams, then forty-three. Adams had been overseeing the day-to-day operations of the department under Douglass, who typically was more interested in the big picture. Adams, a holdover from the pre-Douglass days, had made the transition to the rejuvenated department partly on the strength of his administrative talents. A graduate of New York University School of Law, and formerly an associate at Cullen & Dykman, a well-respected Garden City, New York, firm, Adams had solid credentials as a banking lawyer. He had joined the Chase legal department in 1971 when it had only about ten lawyers.

Another option for Chase was to replace Douglass with a Milbank partner. After consultations between Logan and Chase executives, the bank decided they felt more comfortable with a Milbanker, and partner Ed Shaw was tapped for the job. Within the legal department it was considered a slap in the face that senior bank officials thought none of the in-house lawyers fit to take Douglass's place. Adams stayed on in the number-two spot.

Shaw was a solid choice. Logan was too ingrained in the firm, and he had made it clear he was not interested. Shaw, however, was young and a star. He had a modern outlook, and yet he had been trained by Haberkern. He was steeped in the traditions of the firm, and understood the depth of the relationship between the firm and the bank. Nevertheless, he understood that Chase was becoming more independent of Milbank and he quickly changed his allegiance to the bank.

Early into Shaw's tenure, the Chase legal department grew to sixty-five lawyers and operated much like a law firm specializing in banking. Groups of in-house lawyers handled retail, consumer, international, national expansion, and lending work, as well as regulatory issues and matters related to the operation of the bank. The lending work was mostly limited to simple middle-market commercial loans in which the borrower was not willing to pick up the tab for the legal work. Milbank handled financings in which there were multiple lenders and complex documentation, and the borrower footed the bill.

Shaw increased the bank's reliance on in-house lawyers. He found he could get Chase's legal work done at half the price if he used in-house lawyers instead of outside counsel from Milbank and the other firms he occasionally retained. He figured that in-house lawyers cost the bank about $100 an hour, including salary and other overhead costs. Outside lawyers billed the bank an average of $200 an hour. As he faced pressure from the corporation's senior officers to keep legal costs down, it was clear to Shaw that in-house was the way to go.

"The Chase's needs for legal services has grown dramatically in the last ten years," Shaw said. "A lot of the growth has occurred in the department. While Milbank has grown as well—and while Milbank's banking group has expanded—obviously they would have had to grow an awfully lot faster if we hadn't grown from fifteen attorneys in 1976 to seventy-three [in 1987]."

What stung Milbank's banking lawyers the most as Shaw took control of the legal work was that they could not participate in Chase's national expansion kick. The strategy was the outgrowth of the campaign started by Hammer. The slow deregulation of the banking industry had made it easier for national banks to purchase financial institutions outside their own states.

Douglass was given new, exalted responsibilities as executive vice president in charge of national banking. In 1985, he became vice chairman of the bank. He was responsible for the development of regional banking and leasing, real estate, and trust investment businesses across the country. The legal muscle behind what would become an acquisition spree came primarily from the in-house legal department.

In 1984, Milbank, along with in-house lawyers, had helped Chase merge with Lincoln First Banks Inc. of Rochester, which had over 100 branches. Shaw had been with the bank for only about a year, and the department still didn't have the manpower to handle the deal on its own. For the next two years, however, as Shaw continued to develop the department, Milbank took a backseat role while Chase bankers gobbled up regional banks and savings-and-loans, some of which were casualties of the national thrift-industry crisis.

In June 1985, Chase Bank of Ohio was born with $455 million in assets and twenty-two branches in Columbus, Cincinnati, and Lake County, near Cleveland. Ohio thrifts were in trouble, the result of their inability to compete with commercial banks and their reliance on old mortgages made at low interest rates. Chase exploited the sagging market by buying savings-and-loans, including American Savings & Loan, Tri-State Savings & Loan, First State Savings & Loan Association, Investor Savings Bank, and Mentor Savings Bank. Milbank was not involved. Instead, in-house lawyers worked with Squire, Sanders & Dempsey, a Cleveland-based firm, which assisted with document investigation and legislative matters. Six senior lawyers from the legal department, including Shaw and Adams, shepherded the deal, participating in the negotiations with each of the banks acquired.

Barely five months after the Ohio deal, Chase acquired thirteen offices of three Maryland S&Ls and turned them into Chase Bank of Maryland, with about $700 million in assets. All three institutions, Merritt Commercial Savings & Loan in Baltimore, Friendship Savings & Loan in Bethesda, and Chesapeake Savings & Loan in Annapolis, were troubled, and the deal was riddled with political problems. Adams, along with other Chase executives, conducted sensitive negotiations with the state that led to the merger. A Baltimore-based firm, Semmes, Bowen & Semmes, did the local corporate work. Milbank played no significant role in the transaction.

In February 1986, Chase acquired the Park Banks, its eight branches and two nonservice offices in Florida, from the Federal Deposit Insurance Corporation for $62.6 million. The bank had been closed by the state's comptroller and placed in the receivership of the FDIC. In-house lawyers carried the burden of the legal work on the complex deal, in which Chase became the first bank holding company based outside Florida to be granted a full banking license by the state.

Although Milbank was considered to be forever linked to Chase in the legal and banking communities, some prominent banking lawyers were beginning to notice the legal department's new strength. H. Rodgin Cohen, a Sullivan & Cromwell partner who was an expert in thrift acquisitions, watched Chase's in-house lawyers in action when he was hired by the state of Ohio during its 1985 thrift crisis. "The internal staff probably I saw 90 percent of the time," he recalled. "Chase has really made an attempt to build a top-notch legal staff and I think it's successful." Cohen was also impressed with in-house leader Shaw: "He's extremely knowledgeable. He's really good for his client."

Milbank lost out on some valuable experiences as Chase expanded across the nation. Bank mergers and acquisitions were becoming a hot speciality that incorporated banking and M&A skills. For Milbank, the subspecialty could have been a wonderful opportunity; the partners could have exploited their banking skills and used it as an entree into the mergers-and-acquisitions game. The partners, however, were usually not invited into the acquisition fray.

"Less transactional work comes up to the firm because of the in-house department," conceded banking partner Charles D. Peet, Jr. "But it seems to me the most dramatic example is the decision of the Chase people to do all of the national expansion work in-house. They made that decision early on in the push to national banking. It wasn't taken away from Milbank. It was, in effect, a newly developed area of work that we might otherwise be involved in. We were never given the opportunity to be involved.

"The unfortunate thing from our point of view, is if you are not involved in it on a day-to-day basis, you don't develop any expertise," continued Peet. "You don't get a reputation for being an expert in that kind of activity. When others look for representation in the area they don't think to come to you."

As the Chase legal department became less of an

experiment and more of a fact of life under Shaw, Chase bankers slowly were disabused of the myth that the lawyers upstairs at Milbank were intellectually superior to the lawyers downstairs at the bank. It was taking some of the Milbank lawyers a little longer to catch up.

One of Shaw's complaints was that Milbank didn't encourage bankers to call in-house lawyers. When a Chase banker called a Milbank lawyer directly, Shaw wanted the lawyer to ask the banker whether he had called an in-house lawyer first. "Defining the roles is important and we've made an awful lot of progress," said Shaw. "They used to think that they basically made the decision. We're not asking them to turn down work, but to think of the overall relationship—which is certainly important to them—to keep the overall relationship in mind. . . . I think that, given the historic relationship, there is a little less sensitivity to dealing with in-house counsel than some of the other firms we deal with."

For Milbank's banking lawyers, it was sometimes hard to keep up with Shaw's latest plans for his department. The purchase of the Park Banks in Florida marked the end of the bank's buying spree, and by late 1986 Chase had once again reconsidered its priorities. As usual, the change in course was bound to affect Milbank, Tweed.

Chase—and Shaw—began to push harder into fields historically dominated by investment banks. A setback for all major banks was the lessened reliance on commercial banks by the country's largest corporations.

These companies had once gone to their bankers when they needed an infusion of funds. Now they went directly to the financial markets. The banker who got the call was an investment banker, not a commercial banker.

The Glass-Steagall Act, enacted after the 1929 stock-market crash, had been meant to keep commercial banks out of investment banking. Its drafters believed that many banks had failed because they had expanded beyond their traditional lines of business. But in the mid-1980s major banks launched lobbying campaigns to modify the limitations set by Glass-Steagall, and the barriers began to come down. Although Chase lagged behind Citibank, it developed cutting-edge products that crossed commercial and investment banking lines. For Milbank, this posed new challenges. Milbank couldn't bring enough experience garnered from other client relationships to its work for Chase, in part because of its reluctance over the years to represent investment banks that might have conflicts with the New York Stock Exchange. Milbank was also vulnerable because Shaw was well versed in the firm's strengths and weaknesses.

Some of Milbank's young stars did take on complex work for the bank that required a good dose of imagination. Project finance, the developing and financing of huge energy, mining and industrial facilities, was a fairly new business for Chase and other banks, although the techniques were not so different from those used in other financings Milbank did for Chase. Worenklein became an expert in project financings. He had acquired some of his skills doing deals for other clients, including investment banks.

Milbank was also expert in the leasing area, in which financial institutions bought equipment and leased it back to the seller using complex borrowing and equity investment arrangements. The buyer acquired tax benefits associated with the purchases and the seller received valuable financing. Elliot Gewirtz, a young partner who had captured the leasing work of many Japanese trading companies and banks, also did leasing work for Chase.

But Shaw, his lawyers, and some Chase bankers felt less secure using Milbank on other cutting-edge matters. One Chase officer, after reviewing a Milbank opinion on an investment-banking matter, described the level of expertise as "Investment Banking 1—general stuff, elementary stuff."

"We don't want them to go through the learning process with us all the time," Shaw said bluntly.

Shaw felt new confidence about experimenting with other firms. Once, Chase had always asked Milbank to oversee local counsel's work in other parts of the country. Under Shaw's regime, an in-house lawyer was assigned to supervise that work. Milbank was completely excluded.

Milbank found itself competing with Chase's staff lawyers and with other firms, even in New York. In early 1986, Shaw and one of his senior lawyers, Richard A. Toomey, Jr., did a study of the bank's internal procedures to ensure confidentiality and security in its investment-banking and other divisions. They worried that the flow of information between different parts of the bank that should be kept apart could be a problem. It was a prescient move. Only a few months later Wall

Street's insider-trading scandals would break, underscoring the need for internal security.

Shaw hired Roger D. Blanc, a partner at Willkie Farr & Gallagher, to help review procedures and interview Chase executives. Blanc, a former Securities and Exchange Commission lawyer, was an expert on SEC compliance issues. Moreover, his firm represented investment banks, including Shearson Lehman. He could easily supply the kind of expertise and backup that Milbank could not. Shaw believed that he and Toomey had sufficient inside knowledge of the bank for the study. He counted on Blanc to "come in with sort of a fresh look" at the bank. That was something else Milbank could not provide.

Shaw also passed over Milbank in the summer of 1986 when Chase sold its Computer Power subsidiary to a company owned by Merrill Lynch Capital Partners. Computer Power Inc., based in Jacksonville, Florida, marketed computer software and other services to mortgage companies. Shaw retained Cleary, Gottlieb, Steen & Hamilton, another large New York firm, for the $120 million cash divestiture. Cleary had represented an investment bank involved in an earlier deal when Chase acquired Computer Power. Milbank had never been involved in the day-to-day operation of the company. Shaw viewed the divestiture as "a good occasion to experiment," with outside counsel. In-house lawyer Janet Howard also helped negotiate the deal.

The experiment continued and spread to other areas. For advice on its administration of mutual funds,

Chase Investors Management turned to Brown & Wood, a New York law firm with a group that specialized in money-market and mutual-fund matters.

Puleo and senior associate William J. Mahoney helped Chase's investment-banking arm launch its asset sales business, in which the bank sold loan participations for domestic banks. In 1986, that business grew by 200 percent over the previous year. But although the firm continued to help the bank develop the products, it had much of the lucrative business pulled out from under it. When Shaw saw that the transactions were becoming a routine part of the bank's investment-banking business, he hired a young lawyer from Winthrop, Stimson, Putnam & Roberts and began to do much of the work in-house.

Milbank also lost out in the swaps area. Swaps were a new, extremely complex kind of financing that suddenly became a sexy new tool for commercial and investment banks in the United States and abroad. In these transactions, two companies trade interest-rate payments on fixed or floating-rate loans. They can also exchange payments on loans of more than one currency. In 1984, Chase consummated 150 such deals, generating $4 billion in financings for its customers. The next year the bank completed about 300 swap transactions generating about $7 billion. In 1986, the bank completed about 720 swaps, generating about $20 billion.

Puleo learned the swaps game and did the Chase work for several years. But as the business grew, Chase switched the work to Schuyler K. Henderson, who ran the London office of Chicago's Mayer, Brown & Platt. Chase in-house lawyer Toomey said one reason the bank made the change was that Henderson had been one of the first lawyers to master the highly technical and complex transactions. "I guess it was a matter of going to the expertise," said Toomey.

When Henderson went to work at Sidley & Austin in Chicago, Chase followed. Chase's in-house lawyers felt that Sidley would never take the business for granted. "We have—I won't say a volume discount—but a good rate because of the work, concentration of work," Toomey explained. Sidley billed Chase on an hourly basis, but the charges for junior and senior associates were below the prevailing rate, although not dramatically.

Puleo subscribed to Worenklein's "growth and diversification" strategy, albeit in a less strident manner. And so he followed his own advice: He got himself out into the traffic. He took his swap skills and peddled them elsewhere. To Citibank.

Citibank, like Chase, was increasing the number of law firms it used. Citibank, N.A., North American Investment Bank had retained Cleary, Gottlieb for its swap work. In 1986, however, the bank decided to replace the firm. Shearman & Sterling, Citicorp's traditional outside firm, and Milbank made presentations to a panel of NAIB executives, including in-house lawyers.

Puleo and bankruptcy partner David C. L. Frauman impressed the lawyers with their pitch. Their approach, recalled former in-house counsel Elliot Ganz, who had joined NAIB from Chase, was "very aggressive. . . . You got the feeling that they knew what they were doing."

Puleo had hard competition for the business. A member of the NAIB swap team had once worked at Chase and liked Puleo, but there was political pressure to use Shearman & Sterling. "Shearman & Sterling came with people we basically hated," Ganz said, "and then we had fast Frank [Puleo] come down here and put on all the moves." Puleo got the business. About a year later, however, he lost some of it when the bank hired a group of in-house lawyers away from Chemical Bank to handle investment-banking legal work, including swaps.

Senior Chase executives increasingly viewed Puleo as a valued adviser. He was frequently called in on big-picture issues related to global banking and tough regulatory matters. He was close to Anthony P. Terracciano, the bank's executive vice chairman in charge of the global banking division, which oversaw lending to very large corporations as well as investment and international banking. But Terracciano left to join Pittsburgh-based Mellon Bank in 1987.

Puleo was also often consulted by Wolfgang Schoellkopf, the executive vice president and treasurer in charge of funding, money-market dealing, foreign exchange, securities trading and public finance, and broker/dealer finance matters. Within Chase there continued to be some executives who tried to avoid Puleo, but he had changed. His elitist attitude had softened. Puleo had faced up to Milbank's more delicate relationship with its favorite client.

Ganz knew of Puleo's reputation as "obstructionist and getting in the way," but, he said, "I think he's totally changed. . . . The most important thing about him is he has figured out where the bank is coming from. . . . The bank has different goals and he has basically adapted to those goals."

In late 1985, when Chase had some industrial revenue bonds offerings to assign, the bank's legal department asked Puleo to bid for the work on some of the issues. The idea was to keep the cost down—the legal fees were built into the price to the customer. Chase asked Puleo to come up with a ceiling for Milbank's fee.

The bank also asked Nixon, Hargrave, Devans & Doyle to bid on the work. The Rochester-based firm had traditionally represented Lincoln First, acquired by Chase in 1984. Nixon, Hargrave said it would do the work for no higher than $20,000. Ganz didn't expect Milbank, with its reputation for charging high fees, to come up with a good price. And, in fact, Puleo refused to come up with a ceiling price, insisting there was no upside for the firm. Instead he came up with a fixed price that was lower than Nixon, Hargrave's bid. "It was an extremely good price and it was $4,000 or $5,000 lower," said Ganz. "This was something I never expected from him based on his old reputation."

With great difficulty, Milbank had learned some valuable lessons about their bank. They finally understood that they could no longer take Chase for granted. Nevertheless, carefully guarded statistics showed that the firm's reliance on the bank had dropped, even though the Milbank banking department had grown from four lawyers in 1959 to about seventy lawyers in 1986. In 1984 and 1985, the Chase fees ran a little more than 40 percent of the firm's revenues. Three years later they had dropped to about 21 percent, although billings had actually gone up.

Chase had long paid Milbank a monthly retainer, meant to cover short conversations between Milbank and Chase people in which the lawyers provided routine, often off-the-cuff advice. For years the retainer had grown annually. But by 1986 it was holding steady at $100,000 a month.

"I hope Chase feels the loyalty that we feel toward it," Logan said in 1986 somewhat wistfully. But Logan, Puleo and Forger realized that loyalty would only take them so far. Unlike Haberkern, they viewed the well-being of Milbank, not Chase, as their paramount concern. Puleo and many of his partners at Milbank began to see that growth and diversification had more than one context. Not only did they have to bring in new clients, but they had to continue to cultivate and develop the sources of business they already had.

And since Chase was no longer as predictable a client, new sources of banking business had to be found. If a new client happened to be one of Chase's competitors—well, that was just the way it had to be. Ten years before, Milbank would never have reached out to Citibank. But then again, ten years before Shearman & Sterling would still have had a lock on that bank's business.

Logan made the diversification of his department's client base a priority. Work for other banks, Logan concluded, "was good for the firm and [Chase]. It keeps us sharp and on the cutting edge. It keeps us in the market and we use those skills for our principle banking client."

And the new Chase was happy to have Milbank learn new skills on someone else's time. "They have attempted to diversify and I think that's something we encourage," Shaw said. He pointed out that he had started using Morgan, Lewis & Bockius for mortgage-backed securities work. "If Milbank had done more of that kind of stuff, it would be more likely that we would have gone to them."

Logan targeted international banking as a growth area. Milbank had long represented some prominent foreign banks; it had been easier to represent foreign banks than Chase's domestic competitors. The firm represented Credit Suisse, Bank of Tokyo, Banco de Brasil, and Italian and Dutch banks. In 1985 and 1986, banking partners captured the work of several important Japanese financial institutions and Midland Bank, a British bank Logan spent much of his time counseling.

The relationship between Chase and Milbank was not likely ever to settle into its former complacency. In late 1986, Logan held what he called "a shirtsleeves session" at Milbank's uptown office. The meeting was planned to coincide with the election of partners, an event always deemed important enough for partners to fly in from Europe and Asia. In a Rockefeller Center conference room, Logan mixed banking lawyers with corporate and real estate lawyers. He sat partners with international expertise next to confirmed New Yorkers who were courting foreign financial companies with New York branches. As Logan put it, he "set 'em in a brown bag and mixed them up a bit."

The combined talent of the dozen or so partners discussing rainmaking and business developments was sufficient to meet the challenges of the changing financial marketplace, challenges that Milbank was being forced to face for the first time. This group of lawyers could bridge the gap between commercial and investment banking, combine financial and real estate expertise and exploit global financial markets. All that was required was the managerial and entrepreneurial insight that Milbank was trying to foster in its partners. The meeting was a sign of Milbank's nascent ambition. For the first time, the firm was thinking creatively about its potential. And the senior partners turned to their young colleagues to fulfill that promise.

6

WHIPPERSNAPPER RAINMAKERS

CHASE HAD BECOME fickle, but that was not the only reason for Milbank's lessened reliance on the bank. New business was indeed beginning to flow to the firm. Although Forger and the other senior partners recognized the importance of developing new corporate clients, it tended to be young partners who experimented with rainmaking.

The young partners realized they had to fill the gaps in Milbank's client roster. Worenklein's call for growth and diversification focused their attention on the problem for the first time, and rainmaking became a constant topic of conversation among the firm's emerging generation. Unfortunately, when it came to drumming up new business, they had few role models. Some of the older men who had shepherded these young lawyers into the partnership had even discouraged the search for new business. Partner Anthony D. Schlesinger could still recall a meeting of the partners in the institutional-finance group shortly after he became partner in the mid-1970s. According to Schlesinger, partner Charles D. Kyle told the assembled lawyers, "The telephone is going to ring the same number of times every year no matter what we do." Schlesinger and his fellow young partners were reluctant to offend their seniors by contradicting them. "There always seemed to be enough to fill up the day of the partners, but never to stretch them," Schlesinger said about those times. When young partners did whisper among themselves about developing clients, they talked about taking businessmen and in-house lawyers to lunch.

A decade later, some Milbank partners still considered taking clients to lunch to be a novel endeavor. But a growing number of young partners knew that lunch was not enough. Other firms seeking an infusion of business looked to partners who could be lured from the outside with promises of extra dollars. That was not an easy option for Milbank, however, which still clung to its lockstep compensation system.

And so on their own, Milbank's young partners began mastering the art of bringing in business. These young partners set out to reinvent themselves as rain-makers. They started from scratch; they had no one to look to for guidance, so they molded their image according to their own interests, personalities, and quirks. The style of each partner's rain dance was different. No matter what role a partner chose to play—entrepreneur-ial adviser, salesman, or traditional counselor—it was clear that the game had completely changed since the firm's early years. Nobody hired these young partners because they went to the same prep schools or elite universities. Family ties and fortunate marriages simply were no longer germane. The pitch of Milbank's young whippersnappers was a blatant request for business. They removed the mask of deference and gentility that years of apprenticeship at Milbank had taught them, and openly bragged about Milbank's skill. Hire Milbank, they told prospective clients, and that expertise would be at the clients' disposal; Milbank had something special to offer.

More than one young partner joked that their predecessors at Milbank were likely spinning in their graves as the youngsters openly marketed and strutted their stuff. Yet there were few complaints from the senior partners, who had been convinced by Forger and others that an aggressive sales approach was a must if Milbank was going to keep up with the competition. Among the Milbank partners who transformed themselves from traditional counselors to young power lawyers were Jay Worenklein, Mel M. Immergut, and Kevin R. Hackett. Their styles were different, but each created a routine that appealed to and flattered clients. And over time, the three partners themselves became role models for their senior and junior colleagues.

Worenklein sold himself as an entrepreneurial counselor. He didn't simply document deals, he told his clients. He presented them with innovative possibilities and sometimes even business partners that added value to the pure legal work Milbank performed. He found a way to accomplish what the client wanted done, no matter what the obstacles. Worenklein's rain dance paid off; by 1986, he was generating about $5 million a year in billings, and Chase accounted for little of the revenue.

His booming practice had not come easily. It started with a misfortune that almost drove him from the firm. After having badgered Bob Douglass for the assignment, he spent four years trying to put together ESPRI (Empire State Power Resources, Inc.), an energy consortium that would have financed and built power plants in New York State. When the Public Service Commission killed the idea in 1977, Worenklein was devastated. Almost a decade later, Schlesinger still remembered seeing the downcast young lawyer sitting in front of his secretary's typewriter, pounding out his résumé.

Instead of leaving the firm, however, Worenklein parlayed his experience on the project and as a banking associate into a utility-financing specialty. There was nobody to guide him in the arcane field. Manro T. Oberwetter, who had worked with Chase's petroleum department, had left the firm after the 1967 Arab-Israeli war, when the oil industry collapsed. Another senior banking partner, Michael F. Orr, had taken up the energy mantle, but he had also spent much of his time counseling Chase.

And so Worenklein managed to attach himself to other financing projects that involved energy issues. He represented Dean Witter Reynolds Inc. in several foreign and domestic energy and utility projects, and handled a financing for Tucson Electric Power Company. He spent much of 1979 and 1980 counseling a group of lenders, headed by Chase, in the financing of a $1.4 billion bauxite mine and alumina refinery in Australia. It was a complex, off-balance-sheet transaction in which Reynolds Metals Company owned the project for tax but not accounting purposes. Worenklein was supervised by banking partner Peter Rowntree, but handled the brunt of the work himself.

Already, Worenklein was following an unorthodox career path at the firm. He straddled two departments; ostensibly he was a banking associate, yet he also worked with Lilley, who had his own corporate fiefdom and had supervised Worenklein on the ESPRI project after Douglass departed. While still an associate, Worenklein brought in some work from Salomon Brothers, which had also been involved in ESPRI.

Worenklein seemed never to stop working on projects, both inside and outside the firm. He was billing well over 2,000 hours a year, but somehow found spare time to paint. As his young family slept, he threw large canvases down on the floor of his Upper West Side apartment and crafted stark, abstract pictures. In between meetings in Australia, he took technically proficient photographs.

Partnership decisions were looming. Shortly before the elections, Salomon Brothers offered Worenklein a job. He had received favorable feedback from Lilley and thought he had a good shot at partnership. Still, at Milbank making partner was a mysterious process and it was difficult for associates to evaluate their prospects. Sometimes they were asked to wait another year, with no guarantees. Occasionally, the morning after the decisions, disappointed young lawyers prowled the office, looking for an explanation.

Worenklein didn't want to take chances. Though it was hardly Milbank style, he told the partners he worked for that if he didn't make partner, he would abandon the practice of law for investment banking. On an evening in November 1981, the partnership anointed Worenklein a partner. He was working late and his wife, Marion, took the phone call with the news. He arrived home to find a handwritten sign on the mailbox: CONGRATULATIONS. Worenklein moved into a partner-size office and tacked one of his abstract paintings on the wall.

Even as a young lawyer, Worenklein had a knack for developing deep client relationships. Almost inevitably, loyal clients referred other business to the ambitious young partner and his network of contacts expanded. Slowly he became known as a player in the world of utility finance, project finance, and leveraged leasing.

Citibank became one of Worenklein's biggest clients. His retention by the bank, which usually used Shearman & Sterling, was a fluke. In 1983, only a year into his partnership, Worenklein represented Chase in the $120 million financing of an oil-to-coal conversion project for Tampa Electric in Florida. But as the deal was being put together, Chase pulled out. The bank decided it could not issue a letter of credit to the utility. Citibank stepped into the breach. As the borrower, Tampa Electric Company had to foot the bill for the legal work. The utility was reluctant to pay another law firm to get up to speed on the project, so it asked Citibank to hire Milbank. Citibank agreed, and Worenklein had a new client.

Once the deal was over, Citibank didn't go away. Instead the bank continued to rely on Milbank for utility financing. Worenklein developed close relationships with many officers at the bank, who valued his ability to structure deals creatively. In 1987, Citicorp placed an advertisement in *The Wall Street Journal* touting its $3.5 billion in utility leveraged leases during the previous sixteen months. "Nobody's a better source of power than Citicorp," the ad copy bragged. The legal muscle behind Citicorp on many of those transactions was Worenklein. By the mid-1980s, Citicorp was one of Milbank's ten largest clients.

Salomon continued to be a client with great potential. Worenklein represented the investment bank in oil-rig and coal-conversion-plant financing, and a $27 million co-generation project leveraged lease, among many other projects. At its best, rainmaking becomes a chain reaction and clients refer new clients to a favored adviser. The investment bankers at Salomon were impressed with Worenklein and sent other companies, including Texasgulf Inc., his way.

Salomon also introduced Worenklein to O'Brien Energy Systems, an independent energy company with a market value of about $100 million. Worenklein represented O'Brien in the development of a steam-production plant in downtown Hartford and in other projects. In 1986, O'Brien went public. Milbank introduced the company to Drexel Burnham Lambert, which handled the initial public offering. That was an extra service that a company might not ordinarily have expected from a traditional law firm. Other clients Worenklein reeled in included Los Angeles–based Security Pacific Corporation, the First Boston Corporation, Southern California Edison Company, the Southern Company Services Inc., Morgan Stanley & Co., Inc., and Combustion Engineering Inc.

Worenklein expanded the firm's rainmaking power in 1985 when he helped recruit M. Douglas Dunn as a lateral partner. Dunn had been a partner at Winthrop, Stimson, Putnam & Roberts, and an investment banker at Lehman Brothers before it merged with Shearson. He was also a utility expert, primarily in the mergers-and-acquisition area. When Worenklein was asked by Drexel in the summer of 1985 to handle the acquisition of a power plant, he referred the deal to Dunn because he was vacationing in Israel. The Portland General Electric project set Dunn rolling, and he began cultivating investment-banking clients in the utility area with Worenklein. Dunn's arrival on the scene convinced even conservative partners of the benefits of laterals. At partnership lunches and meetings, partners began to talk of finding "another Doug Dunn."

Worenklein made client development a priority. At meetings with the partners and associates he worked with, he spoke about fostering client relationships. He became a role model even for senior partners who had spent much of their careers serving Milbank's institutional clients.

Worenklein's pitch to prospective clients was not overly salesmanlike. Instead, he talked of his firm with great pride, and presented himself as a problem-solver. With Dunn he paid visits to investment banks and put on informal seminars for bankers on regulatory issues and new financing products in the utilities area. When his clients at Chase, Citibank, Salomon, or First Boston made pitches to their potential clients, Worenklein was often at their side. And he frequently helped them prepare for these "beauty contests" free of charge.

Between 1984 and 1986, Worenklein's client list roughly doubled, and a group of partners and associates began forming around him, including some of the firm's most promising young lawyers. His cutting-edge work also took on a new dimension when Citibank started thinking about going into the nuclear-power-plant business. The bank asked him to draft a memorandum on financings involving nuclear power facilities. After it was reviewed by senior officers of the corporation, including Citibank chairman and chief executive officer John Reed, the utility experts got permission in early 1986 to develop nuclear deals.

Citibank's and Worenklein's first attempt at nuclear-power-plant financing was the 1986 sale and lease-back of the Palo Verde Nuclear Generating Station Unit 2, which belonged to the Public Service Company of New Mexico. In a sense they had to make up the deal as they went along, for the $430 million deal was only the second sale and lease-back of a nuclear facility. A subsidiary of Citicorp Industrial Credit was the lead investor on the deal, and this was the first time Worenklein had been hired by the leasing group of Citicorp. The investors group also included Chase, Mellon Bank Corporation, First National Bank of Chicago, and Beneficial Leasing.

Immediately, Worenklein was put in a sticky position. Citicorp asked Shearman & Sterling to handle the tax aspects of the deal. That meant that Worenklein would be supervising the bank's regular outside firm. On this ground-breaking deal, Worenklein especially wanted to avoid tension with Shearman & Sterling tax partner William E. (Woody) Flowers. To start off the relationship right, he came up with a new letterhead for the duration of the deal. He had his secretary cut Milbank and Shearman & Sterling's names out of each firm's stationery and paste them side-by-side on a new sheet of paper. Worenklein's primitive attempt at design was a signal that this was to be a cooperative venture between the two rival firms. It was the kind of solution

141

that only a partner used to the collegial, noncompetitive traditions of Milbank would devise.

The Palo Verde deal was extraordinarily difficult to structure. The banks were extremely sensitive to liability issues in the event of a nuclear accident. Tax issues were crucial to the deal, and all parties had to be protected in the event of tax-law changes. And finally there were political problems between the financial institutions involved in the deal. All were major players in the sale/lease-back market and several were not pleased that Citibank would act as the chief negotiator on a cutting-edge deal. Worenklein was the diplomatic compromise. He was designated as group spokesman, and the arduous negotiations fell on his shoulders.

The investment tax credits involved in the deal were unusable if it was not closed within ninety days of the date the Palo Verde facility went into service. Brokers involved had said it couldn't be closed within that window. Some thirty Milbank lawyers toiled on the negotiation and documents. And finally, with little time to spare, Worenklein closed the deal.

Worenklein billed his clients about $1 million, including a premium. He was one of the first partners at Milbank to experiment with premium billing. The concept was that if a lawyer creatively helped consummate a deal, his time was worth more than an hourly rate. The premium made up for the weakness in the hourly rate system. Premiums were what made mergers and acquisitions and other highly innovative deals so profitable. And Worenklein's entrepreneurial pitch had proved effective in generating that kind of work.

. . .

Mel Immergut's approach to cultivating new clients was completely different, yet equally aggressive. The young corporate partner's rainmaking specialty was sales. Immergut offered prospective clients a sort of sportsmanship—often deep-sea fishing—that was an updated version of the old tradition of cultivating contacts at exclusive private clubs.

There had always been partners willing to tout their skills to general counsel, said Immergut, explaining his rainmaking philosophy. "There were some people who did it but they always did it thinking, 'Boy, is this the right way to be doing this?' Now we're more like salesmen."

Salesmen. It was a word that no old-time Milbank partner had ever used to describe himself. Immergut typically spent 25 to 30 percent of his time on what was euphemistically called "client development." In 1986, one of Immergut's busiest years, he spent 2,000 hours on client work and billed 1,000 hours to the firm's "office general" account—wining and dining clients and working on the associates committee. Immergut thought nothing of embarking on a three-day field trip just to schmooze with potential clients, and to brag to them about the firm's financial-services expertise. Even if he did no legal work and racked up thousands of dollars in expenses, he viewed the unbilled time as an investment.

"The firm has been good in letting some people—within constraints—do what they do best," Immergut said. And he was good at "people kinds of things."

And so Milbank allowed Immergut to spend much of his time outside the office selling—and playing. Even Immergut admitted that his was not the "normal road." But Forger and the firm's other powers were willing to bet that Immergut's hours on planes and on motor yachts were worth as much to the firm as the time he spent negotiating deals for huge, institutional investors. And except for a brief period during which Immergut tried to develop a specialty in racehorse law, the gamble paid off.

For some reason playing hooky always seemed to pay off for Immergut. In fact, he landed at Milbank because he arrived at his third year at Columbia Law School a week late and was caught. The man who caught him was professor William L. Cary, a former chairman of the Securities and Exchange Commission. It was September 1970. The previous spring, Columbia had closed down early in the wake of protests over the U.S. invasion of Cambodia. Students had been given a choice: accept a pass-fail grade or return to school early the next semester and take finals. Immergut was also studying for an MBA from Columbia and was planning a career as a management consultant. He wanted to improve his law-school grades, so he arranged to take his exams. That summer, college students around the country protested the war and bummed around. Immergut studied for his exams and worked at IBM.

When exams were over, Immergut and his law-school roommate decided they deserved a break—so they left school for a week to fish off the coast of Canada's Prince Edward Island. Fishing was an avocation

Immergut had shared with his father, a doctor, when he was growing up in Sheepshead Bay, Brooklyn; theirs was not the placid sport practiced in hipwaders in quiet streams. The Immerguts were big-game hunters.

On that trip, Immergut caught a world-record bluefin tuna. "I caught a fish that had never been caught before," Immergut said. "Hemingway tried all his life to catch this fish." The author's widow, Mary Hemingway, showed up at the party celebrating the 1,040-pound catch. Immergut's photo appeared in the sports pages of *The New York Times* and *The Spectator,* the Columbia newspaper.

Professor Cary read the press reports and recognized Immergut's name from his class roster. He noted that Immergut could not have been in class if he was breaking records off the coast of Canada. Cary, whose daughter fished, made sure to call on Immergut when the class next met. He congratulated Immergut on catching a thousand-pound "trout," and the two became friendly. Cary prevailed upon Immergut to delay his management-consulting career and practice law. He recommended Milbank, and wrote a letter to Samuel L. Rosenberry, the partner then in charge of the New York Stock Exchange account.

Immergut followed the advice. At Milbank, he rotated through the firm's departments, looking for a specialty, and in 1972 he landed in the institutional-finance group. He was assigned to work on the leveraged lease of an L1011 aircraft, representing an insurance company.

The institutional-finance group was run by three

older gentlemen, Charles Kyle, Sinclair Hatch, and Edward H. Stiefel, whose clientele consisted of large institutions—typically insurance companies—with lots of money to invest in companies that didn't choose to go to the public markets or commercial banks for financings. The three aging partners were, in Immergut's words, "courtly . . . absolutely terrific lawyers, very definitely from the old school." They sat at their desks and "cranked out indentures," he said. They "sat there and waited for the phone to ring. They didn't have any inclination to go out and make it ring."

Hatch, Stiefel, and Kyle didn't always deal well with younger people. There was a perception in the partnership that institutional clients preferred to deal with partners. Nevertheless, in the early 1970s, when Immergut was looking for his niche, the institutional-finance department presented an opportunity for ambitious associates willing to take a risk. The work was becoming far more complicated and the necessity of bringing in associates to do the resulting documentation was bound to increase the group's profitability. The growth and the impending retirement of the three partners meant that there might be openings in the partnership for associates who learned to represent insurance and other companies in private placements, leveraged leases, LBOs, and other complex financings.

Immergut, Tony Schlesinger, and A. Sydney Holderness, all roughly the same age, bided their time in the institutional-finance group. In 1979, the three older partners retired, and the department belonged to them.

They inherited a steady clientele—Equitable, a client since the 1940s, Metropolitan Life Insurance Company, and Mutual of New York Life Insurance. These clients were simply passed on to the new generation.

The difference, however, was that Immergut, Holderness, and Schlesinger were more sensitive to the increased volatility of the legal market. None of the group's clients relied exclusively on Milbank, and the young lawyers understood that it was important to cultivate these clients even if they already had a generation of experience with the firm.

The three senior partners retired at a critical juncture in Immergut's career. He was a senior associate closing in on partnership. That year, his seventh at the firm, Immergut was invited to play golf by Clark Graebner, a former tennis star and a financial printer who often did work for Milbank.

Immergut was reluctant to play hooky for the day just to play golf. He suggested to Graebner that they play with a couple of lawyers, that way there would be at least the appearance of business activity. The two young lawyers Graebner invited were in-house staffers from Teachers Insurance & Annuity Association of America, one of the largest pension funds in the country. On the golf course, Immergut told his companions about his group's work at Milbank.

It must have been an effective sales pitch, because the next day he got a call from the associate general counsel at Teachers, asking him to lunch. The associate general counsel explained that Teachers wanted to expand the number of firms it used. Immergut scared up a senior Milbank partner to accompany him to lunch. "But that's not what they were looking for," Immergut recalled. "They were looking for a young partner to grow with them. We happened to fit the bill."

Having brought in the Teachers account, Immergut earned a reputation within the firm as a rainmaker at an early age and the next year he made partner. Immergut and the institutional-finance group documented countless deals in which Teachers was the lead lender on complicated financings. The pension fund rapidly became a major client of the firm. In the mid to late 1980s, Teachers was typically among the top five to ten fee-generating clients of the firm. "I am proud of Teachers because I feel without question Teachers has become an institutional client of the firm," Immergut said after serving the client for almost ten years.

He never took the client for granted, constantly shoring up the professional relationship by carefully maintaining personal relationships with Teachers' in-house lawyers and executives. He referred to staffers at Teachers as "out-of-the-office friends of mine." He invited them to restaurants, Broadway shows, and on fishing trips.

Over time, Immergut became more convinced that his personal touch—his befriending of clients—was the key to his success. "You get new clients many, many different ways. Quality is one of the things we talk about here. [But] being able to deal well with people is also important," he said. "Clearly it's been to my advantage that I know how to do things outside the office. I have no doubt that what makes some people more successful at attracting clients than any other people—is that they get along with people better."

When Beneficial Finance, a regular client of the firm, got out of the leveraged-leasing business, Milbank lost its work for the company. Immergut, however, tried hard to help Beneficial's leasing experts find new jobs. It was a gesture calculated to generate goodwill. A refugee from Beneficial, Larry K. Morris, who ended up at Salomon Brothers, recommended Immergut to U.S. West Financial Services, which was looking for New York counsel. Immergut thus corralled U.S. West as a client.

In 1987, Immergut represented Wal-Mart Stores Inc., the second largest discount store chain in the world, in the sale and lease-back of twenty-five wholesale stores, a $144 million deal. Immergut was chosen after Salomon Brothers, the investment bank on the deal, conducted a series of rigorous interviews to find New York counsel for the Arkansas-based Wal-Mart. The deal kept Immergut, real estate partner Kevin Hackett, and many associates busy for months.

Even though Wal-Mart and its chief stockholder, Sam M. Walton, rarely had New York business, Immergut saw the company as a potential big player. He kept in touch with the in-house lawyer he'd worked with on the deal and even flew to Bentonville, Arkansas, the company's headquarters. "I just go down there basically to say hello. . . . Keep up a personal relationship," he said.

On one visit, Immergut met Wal-Mart general

counsel Randy Laney, who dealt with hundreds of outside firms that handled everything from minor personal-injury cases to big deals. Laney called up Milbank's name on his computer listing of firms Wal-Mart used. Next to the firm's name were several Wal-Mart codes, which Laney interpreted for his visitor. The codes showed that Milbank was aggressive and communicated well with its client. One particular bit of code—"$ + "—meant Milbank was expensive. The final code was "yes + ," meaning Wal-Mart would be happy to work with Milbank again.

Immergut left Bentonville with no immediate prospects for work, but certain that Milbank would be considered in the future. The cost of his airfare, hotel room, means, and incidentals was picked up by the firm. It was Immergut's own version of R&D.

In 1986, Immergut was a player in one of the year's biggest deals—the leveraged buyout of R. H. Macy & Co. by the department store's management. Immergut was lead counsel to a group of about forty investors led by regular clients Equitable and Teachers. The deal took five months to execute, and about a dozen Milbank lawyers toiled under Immergut's supervision.

The $4.7 billion deal was extremely complex, and Milbank worked with several other top-tier firms. Ira M. Millstein, the formidable senior partner of Weil, Gotshal & Manges, represented Macy's management. Real estate aspects of the transaction were overseen by Rosenman & Colin. Shearman & Sterling represented a special committee of Macy's outside directors. The banks involved were represented by Sidley & Austin. In all, about 200 lawyers worked on the deal.

The all-cash deal, with some ten layers of financings, was certainly the most complicated Immergut had worked on. Even Millstein had misgivings about whether it could be closed. Yet despite its difficulty, it turned out to be one of the most satisfying transactions of Immergut's career. He was negotiating with some of the most respected lawyers in New York, and it was intellectually challenging as well.

Immergut also took pleasure in the attention the Macy's transaction attracted to him and the firm. He was proud that he was helping Milbank meet its goal of being a major player in the legal community's top tier. The LBO was a national event, and Milbank partners couldn't help bragging that the firm had a piece of one of the year's most high-profile transactions.

. . .

Real estate partner Kevin Hackett's rainmaking strategy was the most traditional of the three partners' and was more subtle than Immergut's or even Worenklein's. Hackett's emphases were service and quality. "You just want to make each client feel like they're your only client," he said. Hackett was convinced that goodwill in the marketplace was the key to developing business. He also believed that his reputation for hard work would lure clients to Milbank and keep them there.

"Grinding it out and impressing the other side with your talent and your ability in the real estate area is still the way you manage your clients and get other clients," said Hackett. "You are known by your acts, not by your words."

When it came to rainmaking, Hackett was a conservative. He followed the example of his mentor, Larry Nelson, the gray-haired eminence of the real estate department. Hackett would never describe himself as a salesman, as did his friend Immergut. Instead he relied on good chemistry, and the hope that clients and other lawyers would recognize his legal prowess and pass his name along.

It was an old-fashioned attitude. Worenklein and Immergut took greater risks than Hackett in their early efforts to bring in business. Hackett's contacts were mostly Nelson's contacts, and he never lost a chance to praise his mentor. Even as Hackett established credentials as a solid rainmaker, he closely identified with Nelson.

Nevertheless, Hackett was willing to make a greater commitment to generating business than had Nelson, who was known as a highly-skilled real estate lawyer but had never built a large department. By 1986, Hackett had established himself as a rainmaker, even though he didn't seem entirely comfortable in the role. That was the year he had his first power breakfast. His guest was Gerald D. Pietroforte, a lawyer-turned-investment-banker from First Boston. Pietroforte was interested in buying and selling mortgage-backed securities, which were to be collateralized by commercial mortgages. A former colleague, who had used Hackett on residential mortgage-backed securities deals, had passed on Hackett's name to Pietroforte.

The scene of Hackett's breakfast was the Regency Hotel on Park Avenue, a well-known early-morning watering hole for businessmen and lawyers who more often than not lived in the neighborhood. The goal of the power breakfast, as Hackett persisted in calling it, was to rope Pietroforte as a client. Hackett was a little apprehensive and had brought along several of his partners for support. Among them were Nelson and Robert E. Spring, a bubbling young banking partner who was one of the youngest Milbank partners to be named in the Social Register. At Spring's side was his mentor, banking and securities expert Robert O'Hara.

Hackett arrived at the Regency early, at 7:45 A.M., and was immediately distressed. When he had called to set up the breakfast, he had been told that the restaurant did not take reservations. But clearly the regular members of the Regency set knew something he did not. While he waited at the door, a parade of business luminaries filed into the dining room. Marty Lipton, the powerful takeover master of Wachtell, whizzed by Hackett. So did CBS and Loews chairman Lawrence A. Tisch, who owned the hotel. Hackett recognized supermodel Cheryl Tiegs and baseball commissioner Peter V. Ueberroth as well.

Hackett and Spring were impressed with the lineup, but they were worried. It would have been embarrassing to invite a First Boston investment banker to breakfast and not get a seat. Corralling First Boston as a real estate client, after all, would be a coup. First Boston had a special relationship with Cravath, and the investment bank also used Shearman & Sterling; Skadden, Arps; and Sullivan & Cromwell.

Pietroforte finally arrived, and Hackett's group was seated. At a previous meeting over Danish and coffee in a Milbank conference room, Hackett had talked informally with Pietroforte about First Boston's plans and told the investment banker about mortgage-backed securities work he and Spring were handling for Drexel. That meeting had been pulled together haphazardly. Hackett had cornered partner Al Lilley in the corridor and asked him to come in and tell Pietroforte about the real estate work he had done for Rockefeller Center.

At breakfast, Hackett introduced Pietroforte to the players who would be part of the First Boston team if Milbank was hired. Nelson talked about the firm's work for developer Gerald D. Hines, and Pietroforte got a chance to meet Spring, who would oversee the day-to-day work.

The breakfast was very cordial. As Spring later noted, the coffee at the Regency was an improvement over the brew served up at the previous meeting by Milbank's cafeteria. The chemistry between the lawyers and the investment banker seemed right. Pietroforte made no commitment to the eager Milbank partners, but Hackett left hopeful that they could capture the business. He also left the Regency with what he called a "special card." On it was a phone number so that in the future he would indeed be permitted to make a reservation. The card was not exactly an official passkey to the mogul club to which Lipton, Tisch, and Ueberroth belonged, but it impressed Hackett nevertheless.

Hackett had good reason to be pleased with himself. Just a few days later, Pietroforte called and asked him to take charge of his mortgage-backed securities business. Pietroforte immediately sent over documents drafted by another law firm for review. Hackett told him that the papers were wonderful, but that Milbank could do better.

Each time a company hired Hackett, he viewed it as his own personal triumph. He was a self-absorbed young man, and he seemed to view his clients as proof of his self-worth. It was an attitude that varied dramatically from that of Nelson, who had steered Hackett into real estate after the young lawyer joined the firm in 1974. Nelson's successful career at Milbank had been launched by serving the firm's traditional clients. The first significant matter he worked on was the building of Lincoln Center, the pet project of John D. Rockefeller III. He went on to represent Chase in its marketing of real estate investment trusts (REIT). Only when Chase withdrew from that business was Nelson forced to cultivate other real estate clients. He became known as an expert in air rights after he represented St. Peter's Church in its sale of its air rights to Citicorp for the building of the Citicorp Center. Nelson also did work for Hines and Kumagai Guno Company, a giant Japanese building contractor with New York business.

Many Milbank partners considered Hines to be Nelson's client, but in fact it was Hackett who had lured the developer over Milbank's threshold. It had been a triumph. The client, said Hackett, "legitimizes us in the eyes of the world—that we represent a major developer that's institutionalized." Hines came along at an important time. It was the firm's first major non-Rockefeller developer client, and it retained the firm just when the Rockefeller family stopped investing in large real estate projects. Other firms were better known for their real estate business than Milbank, and it had been easy to discount Milbank's development work because its biggest real estate client was the Rockefeller family. The Hines work put Milbank closer to the standing of Kaye, Scholer, Fierman, Hays & Handler (counsel to Olympia & York Developments Ltd., the giant Canadian developer) and of Charles Goldstein, a high-powered real estate lawyer who moved from firm to firm and finally settled at Shea & Gould.

Hackett had met Gerald Hines in the 1970s when the developer was putting together the Galleria, a shopping, office and hotel complex in Houston, Hines's home base. Chase, acting as a trustee, was a limited partner in the Galleria, and Larry Nelson had supervised the bank's legal work. As usual, Hackett, then a senior associate, was Nelson's chief lieutenant and got to know the major players on the deal.

About a year and a half later, Hines made his move into the New York market. His first project was a building with a controversial shape that would change the city's landscape, the so-called "lipstick building" at Fifty-third Street and Third Avenue. In 1980 Hines called Hackett and asked Milbank to handle the job.

The job kept Nelson and Hackett busy for several years. Nelson quarterbacked the early stages of the project, including the purchase of the land from Citibank; but eventually, Hackett took over responsibility for the Hines account. He oversaw the building's completion and leases with blue-chip tenants, which included the New York offices of Latham & Watkins, a prestigious Los Angeles firm. Hackett saw the building and his representation as a blessing. He was sensitive about criticism of Philip C. Johnson and John Burgee's design and took special care never to refer to the property as the "lipstick building," a moniker disliked by his clients but popular with many New Yorkers.

On January 1, 1982, Hackett made partner. As Nelson's protégé, his candidacy was as close to preordained as it could be at a firm like Milbank, but his relationship with Hines helped pave the way to the golden ring. He was rewarded with partnership after only seven years at the firm, an unusual honor. Among the partners who also made partner that year were Worenklein and Elliot Gewirtz, one of the firm's young Asian experts.

Other clients snared by Hackett in the mid-1980s also brought significant business to the real estate group. Although Drexel was a client of Dunn's, Hackett also brought in work from the investment bank—the purchase and sale of mortgaged-backed securities. The securitization of real estate was fairly new business for investment banks, and involved the sale of securities backed by groups of mortgages—in this case, residential mortgages—purchased from the originating bank or savings-and-loan. At Drexel, Sally Sickles was developing the mortgage-sale business. Her connection with Hackett came indirectly through the Rockefellers: he met her through her husband, Jonathan Green, general counsel to the Rockefeller Group. When Sickles called Hackett and explained that she was trading pools of mortgages, Hackett's reaction was "This is terrific stuff," but he didn't have the securities expertise to do the deals himself. He went downstairs to see "the great man Logan" and asked for a partner—Rob Spring. Within a little over a year, Hackett's team had done over twenty transactions for Drexel. The work, he bragged, was "growing like a weed," and he was just "tickled" to have been chosen by the investment bank.

In late 1985 a group of investors led by Richard Ravitch, former chairman of New York's Metropolitan Transportation Authority, bought the Bowery Savings Bank. Milbank had a tiny corner of the deal: Ravitch had retained a banking consultant to advise him on the transaction, and the consultant, who knew Nelson, had retained Milbank. Nelson put Hackett on the Bowery work. But shortly after the deal was consummated, Hackett got a call "out of the blue" from Ravitch. The two had met only several times but the consultant had apparently spoken highly of Hackett to Ravitch. "I just happened to be the gumshoe to get the call," Hackett explained with satisfaction.

Milbank handled real estate and traditional banking

work for the Bowery. With banking partner Richard J. Wight, Hackett's team represented the bank in marketing and regulatory work associated with setting up home-equity lines of credit and other consumer products. Wight and other lawyers handled lending and banking-regulatory matters. Cross-selling, the spreading of a client's reliance on the firm to other departments, was an ideal way to institutionalize a client and increase billings. Hackett called the banking department's involvement with his client "dandy."

Hackett had great expectations for his new client, but one piece of Bowery business was not the sophisticated kind of work Milbank usually sought out. Hackett was asked by the bank to assume responsibility for the processing of home-mortgage closings. It was hardly the kind of banking work Milbank was usually associated with, but Hackett said he was "tickled" to have gotten the call from his new client. "I was delighted to help them out, an accommodation to the client, delighted to do it," he said. Two other firms also took on Bowery mortgage closings.

Indeed, plenty of money dropped to the bottom line, even though the business was particularly unglamorous. Milbank couldn't charge the new homeowners the way it did Chase or Teachers, so Hackett decided that "the only way [to do it] without opening a window and throwing money out the window was to hire a paralegal." He hired Margaret Reilly, a onetime parochial school teacher who had spent four years as a paralegal at another firm, to run the closings. He moved the operation out of One Chase Manhattan Plaza to nearby 140 Broadway, where three conference rooms were set up for the work, which was billed out at $35 an hour.

Soon three paralegals were doing Bowery work, closing between six and fifteen mortgages a day. They worked off standardized forms, and only unusual questions were referred to Milbank associates. "The mom and pops come and at the end of the assembly line write a certified check to Milbank, Tweed," Hackett explained. Because Reilly ran her show with little involvement of lawyers, Milbank made money on this back-office operation—which was so tiny that some Milbank lawyers didn't even know it existed. Milbank's work for the Bowery generated between $400,000 and $500,000 in fees in 1986. The next year, the client brought in $800,000. In 1988, Ravitch sold the bank to H. F. Ahmanson & Co., but Milbank continued to do work for the bank.

Within the firm, Hackett's productivity became almost as legendary as Worenklein's. He billed more than 3,000 hours a year. For three years in a row he billed more hours than any other partner. One year at a partners' dinner, his wife Connie was presented with a sterling silver frame with her husband's picture in it—so that she would remember what he looked like. "I promised Connie it was the last time I would win the award," he said.

And he did cut down, arguing that churning out billable hours was not the most effective use of his time. "I wouldn't be doing my job right if I did that," he explained. "That was fine in the early years of my partnership. But I have to balance that with client development."

One reason Hackett cut back was so he could spend more time at home with Connie and their new son. But Hackett had learned the art of rainmaking, and he and Connie practiced it in some of Manhattan's nicest restaurants about twice a week. Entertaining is "very important to do in a measured way," Hackett explained. "People like to be treated to places they perceive as elegant." His guests—usually one business contact and their spouse or friend—were on a "regular rotation" for an "evening out to talk and get to know them," said Hackett. "They respond to that, they feel important."

7

ISAAC SHAPIRO
AND THE
YOUNG ASIAN
RAINMAKERS

IN FEBRUARY 1986, partner Isaac Shapiro told his partners that he was planning to leave Milbank. The announcement shook the firm. At Milbank, partnership was viewed as a lifetime position. Departures had been rare and sometimes painful.

Shapiro's announcement sent young and old partners into the depths of sadness, resentment, and anger. To make matters worse, this was not a private tragedy. Shapiro, fifty-five, was leaving for Skadden, Arps, which was enough to make his move a very public event in the legal community. His defection was hot gossip in the hallways of law firms all over the city. The legal press trumpeted the career change of one of the nation's prominent experts on the Far East. It was a setback to Milbank's campaign to repair its image, even though Shapiro was not taking significant business with him.

The move was further humiliating because it pointed to the financial differences between the two firms. In 1985, Milbank's profits per partner were almost $250,000 lower than Skadden's. Shapiro insisted that money was not at the heart of his decision. "At my stage in life, I'm not going to change my lifestyle," he said. The legal community was nevertheless making the financial comparison, and the partners at Milbank knew it.

It was not Milbank style to create a scene when confronted with bad news, and most partners seemed to accept it with equanimity. Still, some seethed. There were grumblings about the firm having carried Shapiro during some lean years. In a way, Shapiro's career was illustrative of Milbank's philosophical tussle with itself. He had been indoctrinated with the old Milbank ways, and had been thrust into the new competitive marketplace with mixed results. He had never successfully parlayed his Asian expertise into a booming practice.

For the partners, Shapiro's departure was frustrating and confusing. Many other partners had helped build Milbank's Far Eastern business, but the world did not know that. While they worried about what recruiting laterally would do to the firm, they never dreamed that they would be vulnerable to raids from the outside. They had made financial sacrifices to preserve the firm's collegiality and in the end the firm's culture and tradition had failed to bind the partners together.

Shapiro had not been looking for a new job when Skadden called. The inquiry was the result of a little behind-the-scenes social gossip. Elizabeth J. McCormack, a friend of Shapiro's, confided to a friend of hers that Shapiro was less than happy at Milbank. The recipient of that tidbit was Robert S. Pirie, president of Rothschild Inc. McCormack and Shapiro were trustees of the Asian Cultural Council Inc., an organization that supported cultural exchange between the United States and Asia. McCormack, a former nun and president of Manhattanville College, was employed by the Rockefeller family, which helped support the council.

Pirie was a former Skadden partner and regular client of his old firm. He knew that Joe Flom, the premier takeover expert at Skadden and the architect of the firm's success, wanted to extend Skadden's sphere of influence to Asia. Pirie suggested that Skadden contact Shapiro, and Skadden partner Mark N. Kaplan, who knew Shapiro from Columbia College and Columbia Law School, said he'd give him a call.

McCormack had prepared Shapiro for the call, so he was not surprised to get a breakfast invitation from someone with whom he'd last shared a meal several decades before. Shapiro and Kaplan met at the Regency Hotel, a short walk from Shapiro's Park Avenue apartment and Skadden's Third Avenue headquarters. Only after they sat down did Kaplan reveal his motives for the meeting. Kaplan tried to sell Shapiro on Skadden, a firm most lawyers would eagerly join. He said Shapiro headed the firm's list of potential candidates to help the firm develop a Far Eastern practice.

Shapiro was not so sure. "My first reaction was it's sort of silly. I'm perfectly happy," he recalled. Nevertheless, he couldn't ignore Kaplan's exhortation that he meet with Peter P. Mullen, Skadden's top manager. Soon he was negotiating in earnest.

The truth was, Shapiro was not perfectly happy. He harbored resentment that Milbank had not fully supported his sometimes unsuccessful efforts to attract a Far Eastern clientele. In 1977, he had moved to Tokyo at the firm's behest to open a Milbank office; but before the branch broke even, William Jackson, then chairman of the firm committee, had advocated closing its doors. Early on, Ron Cullis, the firm's executive director, would calculate how much money would drop to the bottom line if the firm got rid of its overseas offices. "There was a feeling among some of the partners that foreign offices were a waste of money," said Shapiro.

Shapiro felt that if Milbank did succeed in diversifying its corporate clientele, it would help him develop his own business; but he doubted that the firm could broaden its practice to the point where it approached the strength of Skadden's. He wondered whether a firm so closely linked with the banking world could build a substantial corporate practice "without a very dramatic step or a merger."

"I don't think one can shake one's image very

quickly," he concluded. Milbank "hadn't grown through acquisitions of talent like Skadden. The chances of it happening seemed to me to be very slim."

At least one of Shapiro's friends at Milbank also thought that he was feeling increasingly awkward and insecure at Milbank. Forger was slowly pushing the firm toward greater productivity. He was telling his partners that partnership was not necessarily forever. A friend of Shapiro's thought that such talk worried him. "People might take you seriously," the friend recalled him telling Forger. "Or might think you mean it." It was becoming obvious that the advent of merit compensation was inevitable, and that it was going to make things less comfortable at Milbank.

Shapiro's rainmaking was not impressive for a senior partner with a widespread reputation as an expert in his field. "Those qualities were not translated into business development," explained a Milbank partner. Another senior partner said that Shapiro's billings didn't cover his own compensation and his share of the firm's expenses.

Shapiro said he felt his partners did not appreciate "the contribution I made" and pointed out that the firm would not have had a Tokyo office until 1987 if it had not been for his earlier efforts. As an associate, he said, he was more successful than most of his peers at bringing in business. Later, "I felt I was one of the partners better known in the community than a lot of my colleagues," he said, "and I was responsible for introducing clients to the firm, not only domestically but internationally."

(He said that clients he brought with him to Skadden generated "upwards of $4 million" during an eighteen-month to two-year period at his new firm.)

Shapiro's wife Jacqueline came down heavily in favor of the switch to Skadden. After talking to some friends in Japan, and learning that Skadden was widely known there, Shapiro made his decision.

Shapiro anguished over his move. On a weekend in late February, he called Forger, who was busy gearing up for the beginning of the Johnson estate trial which was set to begin the following week. Forger was shocked and upset at the news, but Shapiro thought he was gracious. The firm chairman called Logan, who dropped his usual composure. Logan and Shapiro had worked closely together to build the firm's Far Eastern offices. "Frank asked me three times if it was irreversible. I think he knew the answer," said Shapiro.

Over the previous decade and a half, Shapiro had earned a reputation as a legal expert on the Far East. When Japan emerged as an economic power, he was one of a handful of lawyers at Wall Street firms who knew anything about the Japanese. Shapiro was born in Tokyo to Jewish parents in 1918. His father, who had fled Russia to Japan in 1920, and his mother were musicians. Shapiro lived in Japan throughout World War II, and had no way out after the war ended. His family were not Japanese citizens; they were stateless. Shapiro befriended a U.S. marine and the American consulate created a document to allow him to go to school in the

United States. He earned his undergraduate and law degrees at Columbia and in 1956 joined Milbank, Tweed, Hope & Hadley.

Shapiro spoke English, Japanese, French, and Russian, but his linguistic prowess was rarely put to use in his early years at Milbank. He was a member of the litigation department, where for many years he concentrated on antitrust work. As a distraction from his work as a litigator, he became involved in organizations that promoted Japanese-American friendship. Things Japanese were an interest he shared with one of Milbank's important clients—John D. Rockefeller III.

In 1952, Rockefeller became president of the Japan Society, a cultural group that had been suspended during the war. When the secretary of the organization quit in 1963, Rockefeller started looking for a replacement. His personal secretary had a suggestion: her husband, Henry J. Wimmer, was an associate at Milbank, and the couple had befriended another associate who was born and raised in Japan. Rockefeller called Lockwood, the family lawyer, and asked if he knew a young man named Shapiro in his firm.

Shapiro soon became Rockefeller's protégé at the Japan Society. "John D. Rockefeller liked Ike," said a lawyer who knew both men. Rockefeller, he said, was drawn to Shapiro's unusual background. "Ike speaks good Japanese and he's a personable guy . . . Rockefellers—they take strange interests." Shapiro became one of Rockefeller's conduits of information about Asia. Frequently he was at Rockefeller's side when the philanthropist took annual trips to Japan. At Milbank, there were no complaints that Shapiro was being dragged away from his legal duties. On those forays he met several Japanese prime ministers and the emperor. It was heady stuff for the young lawyer, who made partner in 1966.

Shapiro also rose through the ranks of the Japan Society, which was fast becoming a favorite charity of well-connected businesspeople. In 1969 he spent a third of his time helping run the organization. The next year, Rockefeller stepped aside as president in his favor. When Emperor Hirohito visited New York in 1975, Shapiro was his official host.

Meanwhile Shapiro had all but given up his antitrust litigation practice. To the dismay of Jackson, his mentor, Shapiro decided to concentrate on building an international corporate practice. Unhappy with Shapiro's decision, Jackson partially cut him off from the flow of litigation department work. Some other partners, learning about the split, were also reluctant to send Shapiro business. "I then sort of had to make a new life for myself at the firm," Shapiro said. When Shapiro's partners complained about his lean years, this was the period they referred to, Shapiro believed.

In 1977, Milbank sent Shapiro to Tokyo to set up a branch office. Japanese business had matured and was just beginning to be important to American lawyers. "It sort of caught up with me," Shapiro quipped. It was an uncharacteristically savvy marketing move on Milbank's part, and the firm was way ahead of its New York competitors. Not surprisingly, at the heart of this burst of innovation was the firm's desire to serve Chase.

It had started with Hong Kong. Chase Manhattan Asia Ltd., Chase's Asian merchant bank, had been using Coudert Brothers, a New York–based firm with an international bent, in Hong Kong. But in 1977, Chase Manhattan Asia asked Milbank to open a Hong Kong office. Haberkern, ever eager to meet Chase's needs, supported an Asian office: Chase was expanding in what would soon be known as the Pacific Basin; at the same time, there were signs that Chase's legal business in New York might contract.

Haberkern dispatched Logan, his sidekick, on the Chase account, and Shapiro to Hong Kong to scope out Milbank's options in the Far East. It was clear that a Hong Kong office made good sense. Chase had been doing complex syndicated loan transactions there, but much of the documentation had been done by Milbank in New York, or by the bank itself. A Milbank office in Hong Kong could handle that work and serve Chase's needs elsewhere in the Pacific Basin.

Logan and Shapiro also visited Tokyo in late 1976. A senior partner at Nagashima & Ohno, one of Tokyo's most prominent firms, impressed them with the importance of the Japanese market. Logan and Shapiro returned to New York filled with enthusiasm for opening in both cities. The partnership agreed that it was worth the investment. Shapiro moved to Tokyo. Peter M. Mortimer, a senior banking associate, was elevated to partner and shipped off to Hong Kong.

The tall, blond junior partner had a good-natured zeal for banking transactions. From the start, Mortimer had an easier time of it in Hong Kong than Shapiro did in Tokyo. Work from Chase Manhattan Asia was plentiful. Johnson, Stokes & Masters, a Hong Kong firm that had helped set up the Chase merchant bank, referred business to Milbank. After the first year, the firm's Hong Kong outpost broke even.

It was several years before the Tokyo office was regarded as profitable. (The profitability of Milbank's foreign offices was hard to calculate because some of the work that came into the firm via the branches was executed in New York, and New York referred some matters overseas.) Shapiro's entrance on the Tokyo legal scene was fraught with tension between the fledgling office and the close-knit Japanese bar.

The office's economic troubles stemmed in part from the less-than-enthusiastic reception it got from Chase. In Tokyo, with no Milbank to turn to, the bank had frequently used local counsel, including Richard W. Rabinowitz, one of about a dozen American lawyers who had come to Japan after the war and received special permission to practice. The firm he built, Anderson, Mori & Rabinowitz, was staffed largely by Japanese lawyers.

Shapiro and a Milbank associate handled matters for Chase, the Industrial Bank of Japan, and the Bank of Tokyo. The latter two were also clients in New York, and some of the work for those two banks was referred to the Tokyo lawyers by their counterparts at One Chase

Manhattan Plaza. Generating banking work was not Shapiro's forte. Milbank had never set a premium on rainmaking, and he was, after all, trained as an antitrust lawyer. But Shapiro did try his hand at some bank syndication work. Haberkern's "attitude was, don't worry," Shapiro recalled. There's "no mystery to it."

A more significant problem for Shapiro as he tried to make a dent in the Tokyo market was the uproar his arrival caused among that city's lawyers. He had been issued a visa to work in Tokyo mostly, he believed, because of his longtime connections to Japan. It was a concession that connoted great respect; the Japanese bar had stringent admission rules and it tried very hard—and successfully—to keep foreign lawyers out. Soon after Shapiro's arrival in Tokyo, however, his relations with the Japanese soured. Some members of the bar had expected Shapiro to limit his practice to the representation of Chase. Shapiro denied that he had made any such promise.

Many lawyers didn't want Shapiro and Milbank in Japan no matter what the arrangement. Talented young Japanese lawyers believed that the firm's arrival would encourage the perpetuation of the *junkin* system, whereby the Americans who moved to Japan right after the war had been grandfathered into the Japanese bar as special members.

The "grandfathered" Americans and the Japanese had long ago learned to live together, and they easily joined forces when it came to battling Milbank. In all there were only about 150 American and Japanese lawyers in Japan who had the technical and linguistic skills to represent multinationals in their complex business dealings. They wanted to protect their turf as badly as Milbank wanted to protect its representation of Chase.

The controversy over Shapiro's presence in Tokyo became known among Japanese lawyers as "the Shapiro problem." Rabinowitz, whose billings from Chase were threatened by Milbank's presence, was especially annoyed, said a lawyer with Japanese connections. He encouraged his Japanese colleagues to fight. It was widely believed that Anderson, Mori was helping to bankroll the anti-Milbank campaign.

By May 1977, eighty-seven lawyers had signed a petition demanding an investigation of Shapiro. There was also much support for a criminal complaint charging him with the unauthorized practice of law. The bar association in Tokyo demanded that Shapiro present himself for questioning. He declined the invitation and the complaint was never filed.

Shapiro hired two respected Japanese lawyers to help him with the fight. But the efforts of his team could not prevent the controversy from ballooning into a diplomatic nightmare. The tension came to a head when Elliot Gewirtz, then a Milbank associate, applied for a visa to join Shapiro in Tokyo.

With the correct documentation, it usually took only about a month to get a visa to work for an American concern in Japan. But Gewirtz was forced to wait nearly four months while a quiet but potentially explosive diplomatic drama played itself out. After a month had passed with no word, it was apparent that Gewirtz's application was in trouble.

Shapiro asked McCloy to intervene. With his clout as a former secretary of war and former president of the World Bank, McCloy was able to prevail upon Secretary of State Cyrus R. Vance to get involved. The foreign service officer on the department's Japan desk called the embassy's legal attaché to plead Milbank's case and make sure that it was clear that officials at the highest level of the U.S. government were interested in the outcome of Elliot Gewirtz's visa application. The tactic worked. With diplomatic pressure mounting, the Japanese caved in and Gewirtz was granted permission to move to Tokyo. After one last unsuccessful effort by the Ministry of Justice to get Shapiro to sign an agreement promising he would only do Chase work, the fight was over. Shapiro and Gewirtz were finally free to devote their energies to practicing law.

By the time the problems had been smoothed out, Shapiro had suffered some embarrassing humiliations. His reputation as a lawyer who could unlock doors to Japanese business had been dented. There was another blow to his professional ego shortly after Rockefeller's death in a car accident in July 1978. According to an active member of the Japan Society, Shapiro was eased out of any meaningful role in the Society, in part because of the controversy over his Japanese practice. Shapiro said he resigned as president of the Society when he moved to Japan and that he quit the Society after a policy dispute in 1980.

Back in New York, however, Shapiro's partners were using the Tokyo office as an effective marketing tool. They bragged that Milbank was the only American firm with a branch in Japan—and it remained so for some time. In 1987, after five years of sticky negotiations, American firms were finally allowed to send lawyers to Japan.

Shapiro's little office bumped along with its meager business. Gewirtz soon began to give it some direction. He joined Shapiro only to find that "the Tokyo office was doing essentially not much of much," he said. The banking associate was frustrated. Gewirtz was a soft-spoken but somewhat hyperactive doer. His manner— a combination of cautious conservatism and uncontainable enthusiasm for what some lawyers consider to be unbearably dry financing work—was perfect for dealing with the low-key but entrepreneurial Japanese. Over time, the rainmaking skills of Gewirtz and other young partners would convince the Milbank partners that their international aspirations need not rest solely on Shapiro. The truth was that Shapiro, a victim of Milbank's own complacent ethic, was not prepared for the explosion of interest in the Far East. He was also by training an antitrust lawyer, not a banking lawyer, and there was little need for his particular expertise. Shapiro provided the proper image, but banking lawyers provided most of the know-how. As they gained confidence, they outstripped Shapiro as rainmakers in Asia.

Gewirtz's interest in Japan had been kindled more than a decade before. As a student at Colgate in the late 1960s, he studied abroad in Asia. He enrolled at Harvard University Law School and also at Princeton University's Woodrow Wilson School of Public and International Affairs. When he joined Milbank in 1973, he was put on the Chase account. Under Logan's supervision he drafted loan agreements for financings in Asia and Latin America. He was hardworking and well versed in international financing, a skill that was badly needed in Tokyo to supplement Shapiro's cultural understanding but dearth of technical know-how.

As a fifth-year associate at Milbank, Gewirtz had no experience as a rainmaker. Associates were encouraged to churn out billable hours. They were not supposed to spend valuable time looking for business. Rainmaking was a skill lawyers were expected to miraculously display when they traded in their associate title for a partnership. But in Tokyo, Gewirtz realized that if he wanted to keep up his usual frantic work pace, he would have to go hunting for clients.

The delicate-looking and bald Gewirtz did not exactly come across as a party animal. But he started attending cocktail parties and corporate functions and meeting new business contacts. He got a lead at a reception for Mitsui & Co.: he found himself chatting with Kazuo Hayakawa, a young banker from the Tokyo office of San Francisco–based Crocker National Bank. Hayakawa wanted to get involved in leveraged leasing, which had recently come into vogue in the United States as a way to finance large purchases such as airplanes and ships. Leasing was not yet popular in Japan, and Hayakawa was determined to get his clients interested in it.

Gewirtz had done plenty of complex leveraged-lease transactions for Chase, and Hayakawa started dragging him to meetings to lecture potential Crocker clients. For Gewirtz it was nonbillable time, the kind of investment partners, not associates, made for the sake of client development.

About a year after Gewirtz arrived in Tokyo, there was a big payoff, even bigger than he imagined at the time. When Hayakawa got his first leveraged-lease-type deal, he repaid the favor: Gewirtz was included in the action. The approximately $90 million sale of three 727 aircraft to Continental Airlines was a variation on financings Gewirtz had done in the past. It was structured in a manner never attempted before because it involved yen, not dollars, and Japanese trading and leasing companies who were Gewirtz's clients.

The deal was a hybrid. Gewirtz pulled the documentation for a syndicated loan deal and a leveraged lease out of his files and cut and pasted. The results seemed to fit the needs of all the parties. When word got out, there was curiosity in Tokyo's financial community about what kind of deal Gewirtz had created. After it was mentioned in the local press, the Ministry of Finance asked to examine the documentation, since the agency would have regulatory responsibility for the transaction if it was a loan. The ministry agreed, however, that the transaction was indeed a sale—albeit an unusual one. It got the government's stamp of approval. From then on, Gewirtz had plenty of work to keep him and the Tokyo office busy.

Some 12,000 miles away, Gewirtz's industriousness

was noticed by the partners in New York. In January 1982, soon after the Tokyo office became profitable, Gewirtz made partner along with Worenklein and Hackett. Shapiro returned home and Gewirtz was left in charge. By the time Gewirtz departed three years later, the Tokyo branch bustled with four lawyers, and Chase accounted for only about 20 percent of its business.

Back in New York, Gewirtz continued to represent many of the clients he'd developed in Japan. Japanese leasing companies were opening New York offices. American investment banks were increasingly doing deals using Japanese debt. Over time, Gewirtz represented many Japanese leasing and trading companies, including Marubeni Corporation, Nichimen Corporation, Mitsui Leasing and Development Corporation, Orient Leasing Company, Japan Leasing Corporation, and Tokyo Leasing Corporation. He also represented Citibank, Shearson, and Salomon Brothers in yen transactions. These were the kind of financial-services clients Shapiro had rarely been able to attract.

Milbank's Hong Kong branch also thrived. In 1978, the same year Gewirtz joined Shapiro, associate Warren Cooke arrived in Hong Kong to assist partner Peter Mortimer. It was a fortunate coincidence that both associates had a natural talent for courting business. Cooke, formerly a French interpreter for the State Department, made partner in 1980 and took command of the Hong Kong office in 1983.

An important contact for Cooke was Ray Norton, an executive at Chemical Bank. While still working in the banking department in New York, Cooke had worked with Logan on a project financing in which Chemical was a participant. Norton had been one of Chemical's bankers on the deal; later he was appointed the first chairman of Chemical Bank Asia. Cravath, Chemical's primary outside counsel, did not have an office in Hong Kong, and Norton, who remembered Cooke, retained him in late 1979.

Chemical became a constant source of billings. After the bank pushed agent banks to use Milbank in a syndicated note and loan deal involving in excess of $400 million, more work flowed Cooke's way. He was soon called upon to handle similar complex transactions for banks including the LTCB Asia Limited, the merchant bank of Long Term Credit Bank of Japan, Sanwa, Mitsui, Taiyo Kobe, and Sumitomo Trust, all Japan-based, Christiania Bank of Scandinavia, State Bank of India, NatWest, and of course Chemical and Chase.

Cooke's friendship with a Chase banker led the firm to another significant client. In July 1983 he got a call from James J. Liu in New York. Liu had held a number of international posts for Chase, and had just been hired by a Jordanian bank to run its Asian subsidiary, Arab Bank Ltd.; he wanted to know if Cooke would do its legal work. On the same day Liu flew into Singapore, the bank's Asian headquarters, to assume his new post, Cooke flew in from Hong Kong and they signed a retainer agreement.

In 1985, syndicated loan business fell off around the globe, in part because of the growing Third World debt crisis that was keeping Milbank's restructuring team so busy. Many banks needed more liquidity and preferred holding tradeable assets rather than syndicated loans, which stayed on their books longer. The Hong Kong branch supplemented its usual diet of business with private debt restructurings and workouts. When C. H. Tung, one of the world's largest shipping companies, was $2.6 billion dollars in debt, Cooke was retained to represent the creditors' committee on the recommendation of Chemical, the Bank of Tokyo, and Johnson, Stokes. The work kept Cooke's lawyers, as well as members of John Jerome's New York bankruptcy group, busy for about a year and a half.

The Hong Kong work had spread to New York, where partners were also trying to build Milbank's reputation as an international firm with expertise in Asia. By 1986, 80 percent of partner Guilford Gaylord's practice was attributable to some eight Hong Kong companies, and his work was generating a little over $1 million a year. Gaylord was a member of the Stark group, which was losing steam as its namesake got older and its clients were gobbled up by other companies. His clients included Universal Match Box Limited, which was referred to Milbank's Hong Kong office by Johnson, Stokes; Cooke had passed the client on to Gaylord. In 1986, Universal became the first Hong Kong company to go public. Gaylord also represented Englishtown Sportwear Inc., the company that produced the popular Sergio Valente jeans.

Milbank expanded into Singapore as well. The Arab Bank was taking up an increasing amount of the Hong

Kong office's time, and Singapore was a five-hour flight away. Cooke's team was also serving a Chase operation that was only about an hour's flight from Singapore; so partner David Siegfried was dispatched from New York to set up a Singapore office with an associate.

Shapiro's practice paled in comparison to Gewirtz's and Cooke's. His client base was small. In part, this was a legacy of his midcareer practice-area switch from antitrust to Pacific Basin work. A lawyer who represents Asian clients, or American clients doing business in Asia, has to bring to the table an understanding of the geographical marketplace plus a legal expertise. Few companies seeking to expand their Asian business needed antitrust advice—indeed, with the advent of the Reagan administration, there was little antitrust law to be practiced at all. For the most part, Shapiro's work was consulting. Moody Investors Service, Inc. sought his advice when it contemplated a joint-venture credit-rating enterprise. But eventually the company decided not to take on a partner in its Asian business. He also did work for Moody's parent, the Dun & Bradstreet Corporation. When Equitable Life Assurance asked Japan's Ministry of Finance to approve its sale of life insurance to customers in Japan, it retained Shapiro to act as its liaison with the government. Shapiro's other clients were not big fee generators. They included Mitsui Petrochemical Industries, the Zeiss Group, and the Ise Group. The latter was an agricultural business, Japan's largest egg producer. Milbank helped the company acquire several egg-producing facilities in the United States.

It was hard to fathom why Shapiro didn't attract

more business. "His contacts in Japan were almost at too high a level. He operates in the stratosphere," explained one of his former partners at Milbank. "He knows the head of every major corporation. The people who give out the work are at a much lower level." In fact, when a representative of Kumagai Guno, a major Japanese real estate developer, called an associate at Milbank to hire the firm, he specifically asked to meet Shapiro. But according to another lawyer, Shapiro's role was largely that of a respected dignitary; he did little, if anything, to rope the client. By dint of his seniority, Shapiro should have been the dean of the budding Asian bar. But even though he was a spiritual leader of sorts, he had been outperformed by young lawyers inside and outside his firm.

By 1986, it had become popular for law-firm managers to brag about their firms' Pacific Basin practices even though few U.S. firms had really made a killing in Asia. Explained O'Melveny & Myers partner Ko Yung Tung, the star of that firm's budding Asian practice: "Everybody wants to go into it, but very few have succeeded." Several lawyers had made big names for themselves as Asian experts. Jiro Murase, a respected Japanese-American lawyer at New York's Marks, Murase & White, had a long roster of Japanese clients, including Sharp Corporation, Mitsui Group, Mitsubishi Group, Sumitomo Group, and Nippon Life. Tung and another young lawyer, Alice Young, who left Coudert Brothers to start a New York office for a San Francisco firm, had become the celebrities of the field.

But Milbank had also managed to propel itself into the ranks of firms that did more than just talk about having a Pacific Rim practice. The firm had, in fact, developed a strong foothold in Asia. When the firm's 1985 year-end results were calculated, Cooke had good news for his partners about the Hong Kong operation. "We had represented in transactional work over thirty banks and other financial institutions in the course of 1985," he said he told his partners. "And that's treating all the pieces of Chase Manhattan as one." Each year, the office had shown financial improvement, with the sole exception of 1982, when billings showed a slight dip from the previous year. "That was the height of the uncertainty about Hong Kong," Cooke explained. In 1985, the branch's four lawyers had contributed almost $1.5 million in revenues to the firm, or almost $375,000 per lawyer. That was about $50,000 higher than Milbank's average revenue per lawyer, and even higher than Skadden's revenue per lawyer, which was $300,000 for 1985. Moreover, the year-end results did not include spinoff business that had been handled out of New York.

The growth of Gewirtz's Tokyo-based practice also seemed unstoppable. Since 1980, he said, the volume of his business had doubled every year.

The firm's problem was that its practice—with its roots in Asia and not New York—was a little less glitzy and high-profile than some other firms'. It was a marketing issue more than anything else.

Several months after Shapiro left, when it had become all too obvious that his departure was a public relations and marketing disaster, the former partners apparently tried to make him suffer for the insult. Shapiro's capital account, the money he had contributed over the years to the firm, had been returned to him. But he was owed other money as well. The amount was determined by a formula, a multiple of the departing partner's average compensation over a three-year period. If the departing partner was going into competition with the firm, however, the partnership could vote to suspend the payment.

The clause had never been invoked, and Shapiro had left in April believing he would get his money. But in July, he was told otherwise. "After thirty years I thought I was going to have to walk out of there naked," Shapiro said. It was an unpleasant piece of unfinished business, and Forger turned out to be a hawk on the issue. In response, Shapiro's new partners at Skadden drafted a state court complaint, and served it on his former partners.

Slowly, however, as the humiliation and fallout from Shapiro's departure began to fade, Milbank began to see that it had suffered a setback but not a financial catastrophe. Gewirtz vigorously discounted the damage done by Shapiro's defection. "He represents an artist and a chicken farmer," Gewirtz said shortly after Shapiro made his move. He called his former partner "a renaissance man" and a "scholar." But he was only willing to concede that Shapiro "took his stature with him." For Milbank's bottom line, he insisted, the loss of Shapiro might even be an improvement.

Cooke also understood that the firm would feel no lasting effects from the loss. "It was a blow in the sense that it was a black eye for us in Asia. It was an embarrassment. It was not a real blow, sad to say, in terms of loss of business. Really Elliot [Gewirtz] developed much more business." The realization that Milbank's aggressive Asian strategy was likely to continue to be a success appeared to soften Forger and other partners' hard-line approach to their battle with Shapiro over the money he was still owed by the firm.

The negotiations had been difficult. At Skadden, the case file had been given a code name to preserve its secrecy. At Milbank, litigation partner Adlai S. Hardin had been given the job of responding to Skadden's summons. At one point, the talks broke down completely.

And then one day Forger, on his way to meet a Skadden partner on Legal Aid Society business, bumped into Shapiro in an elevator at Skadden's headquarters at 919 Third Avenue. He invited himself to his former partner's new office, with the Asian art and the photograph of Shapiro with the Japanese emperor newly hung. Shapiro and Forger discussed the problem face to face, and the negotiations got back on track. In December 1986 an agreement was finally struck. Shapiro got over half the money due him, but on an expedited, six-month timetable. He was finally able to cast off his Milbank ties.

But his old firm had gained something as well. The partners now understood that their Asian practice hinged not only on Shapiro, but on a handful of young lawyers with a burgeoning talent for bringing in clients. The Milbank partners had also learned that collegiality was not necessarily a goal in itself. The departure of a partner was an unpleasant but not necessarily long-term loss. The firm had learned to live with the unthinkable.

8

THE
RETREAT

FOR ALEX FORGER, running Milbank, Tweed was increasingly frustrating. More and more he saw his leadership role as a burden. Some of his complaints in 1985 were personal. From the start of his career, Forger had always divided his professional life into three parts: serving his clients, bar-association activities, and public-service work. It was a source of annoyance to the chairman that his Milbank responsibilities were taking time away from those other interests. He was putting in marathon days, but he felt he was making only incremental progress toward his goals for the firm. At the point in his career when most partners begin to cut back, he usually arrived at Milbank at 7:30, and was at his desk fourteen hours later, the forty-minute commute to Larchmont still ahead of him. He was putting in sixty- to seventy-hour workweeks and devoting only about fifteen hours of it to non-Milbank work.

Forger was overseeing a staff of almost 1,000 partners, associates, secretaries, paralegals, administrators, accountants, financial analysts, messengers, word processors, proofreaders, recordkeepers, bill collectors, computer technicians, chauffeurs, and maintenance and security staffers who worked at One Chase Manhattan Plaza and Milbank's other offices. At the same time, as chairman of New York's Legal Aid Society, he was immersed in a fight to meet the ever-increasing needs of the indigent with the dwindling number of lawyers willing to work for less than a third of what Milbank's associates were paid. In 1984, soon after he was appointed chairman of Milbank's firm committee, he helped Legal Aid through a protracted negotiation with the lawyers' union. A year later, he arrived at Fordham University for a Legal Aid board meeting only to find 250 pickets— Legal Aid lawyers protesting ballooning case loads. "Luckily," he said grimly a few days later in the safety of his office at Milbank, "they're not unionized down here."

Forger attributed most of his job dissatisfaction to the difficulty of guiding seventy-two partners, each with a theoretically equal say in the firm's operation. Although inroads had been made in business development, and Doug Dunn's arrival had convinced some skeptics that the partnership could benefit from lateral hiring, Forger knew he hadn't pushed the firm toward a more prosperous future, and it worried him.

He was keenly aware that it would be easier to implement his decisions if he were chairman of a corporation and not a partnership, which is bound together not only by business interests but by friendship as well. "Personal relationship doesn't lend itself easily to corporate directive," he said wryly. He dealt with that dilemma by building a consensus for every major decision he made. But even Forger admitted that consensus-building could be "painful," especially when a good many of his partners were "angry about the changes in the profession and want to resist."

By mid-1985, Forger was convinced of the inefficacy of his administration at Milbank—and the eight other members of Forger's firm committee had reached the same conclusion. "Deliberations on any topic frankly just took forever," recalls one member. A meeting in which three issues were on the agenda could take three hours once everyone had made his five-minute speech. Rarely could all nine members attend a meeting. What resulted was almost comedic. A decision would be made at one meeting; at the next, a whole new set of members would revisit the issue. That fall, Frank Puleo, the committee's young banking partner, gave Forger a *New Yorker* cartoon that seemed to sum up the committee's problems.

The multipaneled drawing showed a racing shell. After a splash of vigorous stroking, the boat switched directions.

"We would search and struggle through each issue," Forger said. "We would dissect and analyze and worry and mediate over every issue." Added Cullis: "Alex always gets there in the end. It's just painful."

The torturous route to the firm committee's decision about opening a Los Angeles branch was typical of Forger's reign until 1986. Worenklein had proposed a Los Angeles outpost almost immediately after his appointment to the firm commitee. He had written up a proposal and presented a financial analysis of the potential investment required to make it work. At firm-committee meetings Worenklein pointed out that Los Angeles had become one of the world's most important financial centers and a jumping-off point for doing business with Asia.

It was not a decision to be made lightly. Worenklein predicted the startup costs to be about $3 million, as the branch could not be expected to break even the first year. The money, moreover, would come out of the partners' pockets.

Money was not the only obstacle to opening in L.A. The necessity of recruiting lateral partners to staff the office remained unpalatable to many in the firm. Worenklein's ideas for merging with West Coast firms only increased their resistance, and it soon became clear that the only way Milbank's partnership would open a Los Angeles branch was if the firm committee put together a hybrid staff—part lawyers imported from the New York office and the rest lateral hires.

Meanwhile, other New York firms were flocking to L.A. with mixed results. Some branches, like that of Hughes Hubbard & Reed, bumped along without much success. Sullivan & Cromwell and Shearman & Sterling had made halfhearted entries into the L.A. market. Others—typically firms that had made large financial and personnel commitments to developing the frontier— were thriving. In 1985, less than a year after its opening, Skadden, Arps's L.A. office was handling deals similar in magnitude to those conducted by the firm's Manhattan headquarters. Skadden also picked off some of Los Angeles's biggest legal names. In a less competitive era, Frank Rothman, who had helped build the L.A. firm Wyman, Bautzer, Rothman & Kuchel & Silbert, would have been expected to rejoin that firm when he left his post as chairman of MGM/UA; instead, he negotiated a deal for over $1 million and joined Skadden. Skadden also lured real estate star Richard S. Volpert away from O'Melveny & Myers, a firm that had been considered invulnerable to such an attack.

Forger was solidly in Worenklein's camp. So was Logan, who was convinced that if the firm expanded its representation of banks to regional and international financial institutions it would both supplement and bolster the delicate Chase relationship. But others on the committee wavered. Lilley, a deliberate, practical lawyer and manager, had to fly to Los Angeles with Worenklein to meet with clients and potential clients to ease his skepticism. Jerome was not inclined to make an expensive move that would inflate the partnership ranks with lawyers he hadn't come up with. Reilly, whose mind was on the upcoming Johnson trial and not on firm management, never had much use for branch offices. He saw no reason to change his mind now.

Despite evidence that there were riches to be mined west of the Mississippi, Worenklein's crusade was slow going. For over a year the firm committee debated the pros and cons of a move to California. "We have no reason to be in Los Angeles in 1985," Worenklein said he told his partners. "We're in Los Angeles for 1995. Our clients are decentralizing and we're going to decentralize."

In the late fall, when Forger put Los Angeles on the committee's agenda again, Worenklein pushed for a vote. At the meeting he told his colleagues, many of whom were at least a decade older than he, that he wasn't going to bore them with the details—they knew his proposal: "I said, 'The time has come to make a decision.' " After over a year of discussion, Worenklein's proposal was finally supported by most members of the firm committee. Now the committee would have to start building a consensus in the partnership for a move to L.A. It was still uncertain when it would go before the full partnership for a vote.

The answer to his problems, Forger felt, was a partnership retreat planned for March 1986. According to the scenario plotted by Forger and others on the firm committee, the meeting would be the equivalent of a constitutional convention to revamp and streamline the firm's management.

Coming up with an agenda for the retreat was easy. There were two obvious items to be dealt with: cutting the size of the firm committee to a core group of managers responsible for the firm's operation; and instituting some form of merit compensation. The first matter was easy—all nine members wanted their committee abolished. They lobbied for a three-person firm committee, elected by the full partnership, with extensive power. It would be a Milbank first; the firm had never held an election.

Merit compensation was a more sensitive matter. Forger and Worenklein believed that lockstep needed an overhaul. Logan, Lilley, and Puleo—the less radical progressives—didn't want to completely revamp the system, but they did want a measure of merit introduced into the compensation system. Jerome, even though he was beginning to see that sentiment for change was growing, had major reservations. Russell Brooks, a recent replacement for Reilly, who had rotated off the committee, was more open-minded.

It had been roughly eighteen months since the 1984 meeting at which merit compensation was discussed by the full partnership. Back then even Forger had raised his hand when Jerome suggested tabling the motion. In the ensuing months, however, the partnership's view had begun to shift. This was due largely to a new trend in New York and other major cities. In the 1970s and

---

early 1980s, competition among firms for talent had existed primarily at the law-school level. Until the mid-1980s there had been little competition for senior partners. Big-firm partners were largely immune to overtures from the outside; most stayed put for life. The major exception to this gentlemen's agreement was Finley, Kumble, Wagner, Heine, Underberg, Manley & Casey.

Finley, Kumble was known—and feared—for using big money to lure rainmakers away from other firms. Marshall Manley, one of Finley, Kumble's managing partners (and himself an alumni of a prestigious Los Angeles firm), had developed a reputation as an intrepid raider—the legal equivalent of a Carl Icahn or Saul Steinberg. He argued that the bonds between partners were more financial than personal. When a partner defected, Manley believed, it was simply because the firm was not meeting his economic needs. Loyalty had no place in the equation.

Such an attitude was shocking to partners in older firms like Milbank. Finley, Kumble's exploits were the subject of derision and the target of much joshing. At a law-firm-management seminar, Lloyd N. Cutler, Jimmy Carter's former White House counsel, joked that Finley, Kumble issued a firm tie so its partners could recognize each other. His audience laughed knowingly.

But to the dismay of many lawyers, Finley, Kumble's forays for talent had simply desensitized the issue. Cherry-picking, as partner-robbing came to be called, was becoming accepted business strategy. The rapid

---

growth of most firms required constant infusions of business. Rainmakers were in demand. Skadden had become as aggressive in its lateral hiring as it was in its takeover practice. Prestigious firms in every city—Gibson, Dunn & Crutcher in L.A. and Dewey, Ballantine in New York—joined the partner-stealing game. And often, old-line firms with lower compensation were the victims.

Of course there were firms that refused to enter the fray. Under the leadership of corporate partner Samuel C. Butler, Cravath continued only to make partners out of its own ranks. But Cravath, with a healthy mergers-and-acquisitions practice and litigation stars such as Thomas D. Barr and David Boies, could afford to stick to its old ways. Milbank, however, could not ignore the trend; the firm badly needed to supplement its institutional clients and the new clients generated by its young partners. It had to have rainmakers and it didn't have the luxury of waiting for more of them to emerge from its own ranks.

Reluctantly many of the partners had come to see that they had to bring in partners from the outside. Although headhunters had been put to work in New York, Washington, D.C., and Los Angeles, the firm's success at recruiting top rainmakers had been very limited indeed. Milbank simply wasn't willing to come up with the dollar amounts necessary to attract real superstars. "We are talking to people who are making a fortune at their firm," Worenklein bragged before the retreat. "So far we've found that our lockstep is no impediment. . . . People aren't that interested in money."

But Worenklein was being coy. Perhaps partners were willing to talk about taking cuts in pay, but they rarely took them. There was no question that lockstep was hurting Milbank's recruiting efforts. In late 1985, Milbank had tried and failed to attract a high-profile trade group to its Washington office. The group, led by Alan W. Wolff, rebuffed the overture in part because its members were turned off by Milbank's allegiance to lockstep. Dewey, Ballantine, the firm the group joined instead, had replaced lockstep with a merit system.

In February 1986, the partners got another reminder that lockstep was no longer serving them well. From the start of his tenure as chairman, Forger had talked about launching a public-finance practice at Milbank. It was a goal that was not easily accomplished from within. Lawyers specializing in municipal bonds have to be listed in the Red Book, a highly selective compilation of lawyers approved by bond issuers. Shortly before the retreat, Forger had started negotiating with Robert S. Amdursky, head of Willkie Farr & Gallagher's municipal finance group. The talks hit a snag in part because the partners were unable to agree on compensation and Amdursky's lawyers in the end decided to stay at Willkie Farr.

In early 1986, however, even with several aborted courtships behind them, it wasn't clear that Milbank would alter its beloved lockstep. Even Oresman was nostalgic about the old system. "If I had my druthers," he said, "if things were the same as they were in 1958 when

I became a partner, I might not have voted for a change."

Forger and his team were determined that this time around the partners would be ready to tackle the issue. They did not want a replay of the 1984 meeting, when the suggestion that a merit component be added to the system had sent partners into a frenzy. In the weeks before the retreat, drafts of the committee's proposal were distributed to the partnership and the chairman invited small groups of partners to a series of breakfasts to discuss the proposed changes in governance and compensation. "One of Forger's great strengths as a leader," said a young partner, "is keeping partners involved with the process." In effect, Forger was telling his colleagues that "growth and diversification" would be a meaningless slogan if they did not clean house and put the firm on a footing to take advantage of new business opportunities.

Forger was chief architect of the compensation plan. He and his fellow committee members knew that there would be little support for a system that was radically different from lockstep. They remembered all too well that two years before the mere mention that objective criteria be used to determine a small component of compensation had upset the partners. Therefore, at the Monday partnership lunches and in the early-morning discussions that Forger led, he chose his words carefully. His key word was *modify*. Lockstep would continue to be the foundation of Milbank's compensation system, but it would be "modified." A compensation committee would only raise overachievers and lower underachievers.

The partners seemed to agree that a smaller, elected firm committee was a good idea. Their attitude, according to one partner who attended the meetings, was, "We want a leadership group. We want you to act like leaders." At the same time, the partners didn't want all their power usurped by a small group of heavies. In response to these worries, the firm committee added the approval of major capital expenditures and new offices outside New York to the list of issues still to be decided by the full partnership.

Just before the retreat weekend the partners received a weighty package which included a history of the firm's governance, information about how other firms ran themselves, and a list of partners, their ages, how many hours they billed a year, and their compensation. Two four-page memos, one on compensation drafted by Forger, and a Puleo memo concerning the new managerial structure, were also included.

Arrowwood is a conference center for major corporations in the New York metropolitan area. Surrounded by sweeping lawns, tennis courts, and a swimming pool, it is equipped with large meeting halls, small rooms for "breakout" discussions, and sleeping quarters for participants. The unobtrusive staff provides the endless supply of ice water and hot coffee that always seems necessary for intense business discussion. Here, companies have been restructured, staff morale has been lifted, and sales forces spurred on. On the weekend of March 7, 1986, Arrowwood was the scene of Milbank's retreat.

That Friday night almost eighty Milbank partners traveled to Westchester County. Some drove their own cars and others shared radio cabs. David Siegfried, the sole partner in the Singapore office, and one of five partners who arrived from foreign offices, flew thirty hours to join his partners. Only dire business matters kept partners from attending. Ed Reilly and his sidekick Charles G. Berry skipped the weekend because they were too immersed in the Johnson estate trial to attend.

Forger had planned to make his opening remarks on Friday evening, but the day before the retreat he had been approached by Larry Nelson, the head of the four-partner real estate group. Nelson was unhappy about the committee's recommendation that a merit component be added to lockstep. He was convinced that the firm's collegiality would suffer irreparable damage if lockstep were toyed with. While Nelson didn't have a band of rabble-rousers in tow, it was obvious that he spoke for a good many partners. In the Milbank tradition of letting everyone have their say—even if it was contrary to the best interests of the leadership and even the firm—Forger told Nelson that the floor would be his on Friday night at Arrowwood.

As clear as it was that Nelson was expressing the sentiments of other partners, it was equally true that he came forward not out of fear for how a merit system might affect him personally, but out of loyalty to Milbank. Nelson had built his sixteen-lawyer group into one of the firm's most profitable divisions. On average his real estate associates billed more hours than their peers in other groups and departments. No one could call Nelson a slouch.

Larry Nelson had graduated from Lawrence College and gone on to New York University's law school, which in the 1950s was not quite the respected school it is today. At Milbank, he had been assigned to the real estate section of the corporate department, and there he had stayed for over thirty years.

Nelson wrote his speech with care. When it was done, he gave the twenty-one-page draft to his protégé, Kevin Hackett, to review. "If I had been asked to sign what he wrote I would have as a concurrent opinion," said Hackett. "I just thought honor was enough to get you through and to pull up the socks of the laggards and reward those who are doing a terrific job, that honor and pride of the firm would be sufficient."

And so Milbank, Tweed's retreat began with an entreaty from the loyal opposition. On Friday night, Nelson stood before his partners, some of whom he'd grown up with, others whom he barely knew. The speech was too important to ad-lib, he decided. He read it.

No less than the future of the firm was at stake, Nelson told his partners. They were deciding something far more important than whether the size of their paychecks would be determined on the basis of what year they graduated from law school or their productivity. He was convinced that a switch to merit compensation would have dire consequences. True, he admitted, the word *collegiality* was overused. But so was the expression *perceived inequity*, which had come into vogue as a rallying cry for the merit-compensation radicals. Nelson recalled that, years before, when he was a young partner, he had lunched with name partners John Jay McCloy, Harrison Tweed, and Morris Hadley. He recalled that they had treated him as an equal simply because he was their partner. Some of the firm's most eminent partners of old, he reminded his audience, were not big producers of business but had nevertheless been valued for their impressive knowledge and skill.

Lockstep compensation allowed partners to focus on serving their clients instead of amassing power, he argued. He painted a picture of life without lockstep, a world with squabbling partners, unbridled quests for power, and partners deserting the firm solely for more lucrative opportunities. In short, money ruled, and, as Nelson reminded the quiet group before him, quarrels over money inevitably brought out the worst in people.

The rules were changing, Nelson said, and the good-spirited camaraderie that made team play successful was in jeopardy. Nelson turned to Hackett, who was sitting among the other listeners, and told him he was dumb. The effect of the accusation was startling, and it was calculated to be so. Hackett, Nelson explained, had joined the partnership content that his professional life would be infused with the goodwill and collegiality that a Milbank career had always promised. His protégé had been as foolish as he was to assume that that would never change. The young real estate partner, Nelson continued, would benefit from a merit system. But he questioned whether Hackett was more deserving than the other members of the 1982 partnership class: Worenklein, Gewirtz, and Douglas W. Jones, a busy corporate partner. Milbank partners had always competed with lawyers outside the firm, Nelson concluded. But under a merit compensation system, they would be forced to compete with each other.

When Nelson stepped away from the podium to thunderous applause, Worenklein suddenly wondered if the firm committee plan wasn't headed for disaster: "I thought, 'Oh my God.'" Forger's carefully thought-out scenario was threatening to spin out of control.

Nelson's passion impressed nearly everyone. "Only when I got to the retreat was I treated to the full range of opinions," said Joseph S. Genova, a litigator who had made partner in January. Genova wondered "whether I had gotten on the boat just in time to see it wrench itself in half."

After Nelson spoke, Lilley reported to the partnership on the history of the firm's governance, and Cullis gave a summary of the firm's growth and finances during the past three decades. After the meeting broke up and most partners went to bed, some of Nelson's sympathizers stayed up past two A.M., drinking and debating the demise of lockstep.

In a firm where votes were simply tallies of who was for and against a motion, Nelson might have spent the night soliciting support. At Milbank, however, a consensus included those who reluctantly agreed that a peaceful solution was best. In the morning at breakfast there was no incipient rebellion. There was, however, much apprehension about the coming day's events and the potential for the kind of dissidence between partners that Milbank had always tried to avoid. Forger's antidote to those fears was a poem he had written several hours earlier. He began Saturday's session by reading his partners a playful account of the last twelve hours. The poem's tone was gently humorous. It elicited a few chuckles from the partnership. The mounting tension in the room began to dispel. "One just tries to keep a light touch," Forger said.

Forger was master of ceremonies for the rest of the day, and from then on, the retreat belonged to him. As he led the partners through easy and potentially explosive issues, he managed to keep the emotions of almost eighty partners in check.

His strategy was to dilute the big decisions by breaking them down into tiny ones, and then conducting what seemed like a countless number of votes. After running through the committee's recommendations, he started with a vague, yet crucial, question. Who, he asked, believes that the present system of compensation should be kept intact, without any change? Forger had the venerable seniors, Oresman and Jackson, count hands. Only a small number went up. Roughly seventy partners felt that some modification was necessary. "That set the stage," said Worenklein. "Nobody felt that lockstep was ideal. I just thought it was brilliant."

Next the partners were divided into "breakout" groups, a well-known technique used at retreats to air topics at meetings too large for one discussion. Partners had been assigned groups ahead of time by Forger and Cullis, who had read up on retreat techniques and run them at his previous companies. They selected chairmen, typically respected partners with moderate viewpoints. Carefully, they mixed and matched partners. Each group was made up of eight to ten partners from various departments and different age groups. The groups were politically diverse as well. The Hacketts were separated from the Nelsons, and the Worenkleins from the Forgers. Finally, a partner from the firm committee was assigned to each group to make sure that the committee's view was adequately represented—and firmly pushed.

The breakout chairmen reviewed the recommendations with the partners, asking them to debate guidelines and voice their fears and concerns. Recurring themes emerged. Puleo's memo recommending a three-member firm committee seemed too small a number to some partners, who also questioned his suggestion that the three-person committee select its chairman. It was an important issue. Traditionally the chairman of the firm committee had acted as the leader of the firm. He was a man everyone would have to live with, and the partnership wanted a voice in his appointment.

On the compensation front there were few details to debate. The firm committee had avoided setting out specific guidelines for how compensation would be awarded or taken away. One comment, which seemed to crop up often in the discussions, surprised members of the firm committee: There seemed to be widespread belief within the partnership that it had always been within the firm committee's power to chop the pay of severe underproducers and raise the pay of overachievers. Nevertheless the partners made it clear that they didn't want changes in compensation made on the basis of only a year or two of strong or weak performance. A highly productive partner would not be penalized for a bad year. Compensation was only to be adjusted after years of lackluster or superior work. Untimely tampering was tagged "tinkering"; not even the Lilleys, Oresmans, and Worenkleins wanted that.

Worenklein had been assigned to a conservative group. Its chairman, Tony Schlesinger, was a member of the institutional-finance group. Although he wasn't considered one of the firm's superstars, no one could question his credentials as a hard worker. Schlesinger supported the firm committee's proposals, as did Peter Mortimer, who had done a tour of duty in Hong Kong and now headed the London branch.

But perhaps the group's bellwether was Samuel S. Polk, descendant of President James K. Polk. Though the trusts-and-estates partner was considered to be conservative on firm matters, he was highly respected by his colleagues for his pragmatic, well-tempered thinking. Polk was a likeable guy, and he was often designated for midmanagerial posts such as chairman of the legal personnel committee, which oversaw associate evaluations and salary schedules—ticklish matters that required a steady hand. Polk supported the modified lockstep. "I really think it was time for a change," he said.

Other cautious members of the group, however, were worried. Trusts-and-estates partner Carolyn C. Clark divided her time between servicing not-for-profit organizations and younger members of the Rockefeller family. She found the specter of merit compensation unsettling and lobbied for departmental representation on the firm and compensation committees.

Burt J. Abrams, recruited from the Justice Department years before to fill the firm's never ending need for tax experts, was a slow and deliberate thinker and worker. Abrams, also a conservative, suggested that only members of the senior class of partners be adjusted, and that the bulk of the partners be left in their seniority-determined tracks.

Frank Musselman, the firm's former managing partner from the days when Haberkern chose not to busy himself with the more mundane aspects of day-to-day management, was also wary of the plan. He believed that the compensation committee had to look beyond billable hours at nonchargeable time and whether those hours were wisely spent. Most of the partners in the group thought that only overachievers should be moved on the compensation scale, and only in extreme cases. Worenklein, of course, did not subscribe to the majority opinion. He thought partners should be moved up and down.

Banking partner Joseph R. Siphron led another group. Like Schlesinger, Siphron had clearly been selected by Forger and Cullis because of his reputation as a moderate. In his group, which was more balanced than the one Polk and Worenklein were in, Jerome and trusts-and-estates partner Carroll Wainright advocated staying with lockstep; Japan expert Gewirtz and institutional-finance partner Immergut championed the merit system. "Two years ago I was very strongly in favor of keeping the lockstep system we had," Immergut explained. But as the firm grew, and as he started seeing it as a business, Immergut began to change his mind. He saw "that we are going to have to be taking in larger and larger numbers of lawyers. There's going to be variation in the quality of people brought in. We've got to have some way to make distinctions."

As another group mulled over the consequences of the change in governance and lockstep, Joe Genova, one of the firm's youngest partners, regained some of the confidence in the partnership he'd lost the night before. He felt that his group, which included former chairman Bill Jackson, who said little, Singapore-based Siegfried, and banking partner Jeffrey Tallackson, generally supported the proposed changes. "Things began to come together," Genova said. "The tales of horror that Larry [Nelson] had so eloquently described wouldn't necessarily follow. This change would not be without risk. This is not an easy decision, but fundamentally we believe in ourselves. If we were sharks, kept at bay by lockstep, we don't have much to lose anyway."

At the end of the morning, a survey was distributed listing alternatives to the firm committee and lockstep. The partners were asked to check their preferences. As Cullis and Jane Lawther MacLennan, an administrator who assisted the firm committee, tallied the surveys, the partners broke for lunch.

After lunch the partnership voted on the issues. Over the course of the afternoon, Forger asked Oresman and Jackson to count hands some thirty times. Milbank's new governance was put together like a puzzle. Forger started with the less controversial issues—such as the creation of the new slimmer firm committee. "Here were nine respected people in the firm who were coming back and saying we feel it can be more effectively done by a smaller group of people and we're telling you that unanimously," said Immergut. "It's hard to fly in the face of that."

The partnership approved the formation of a three-member committee even though there had been widespread sentiment for a five-member committee. As Forger moved on, the makeup of the compensation committee was questioned from the floor. The proposal was that the new committee be composed of the three firm committee members plus two additional members elected by the partners. Why not have two entirely separate committees? some partners asked. The suggestion was almost unanimously defeated, as was departmental representation. The firm committee only lost on one point: the partnership voted to reserve the power to elect the chairman of the committee for itself.

Milbank's new governance was being sculpted almost exactly to Forger's specifications. The firm committee even had a new name—the "executive committee." Without thinking, Puleo had used that term in his memo, and it was almost unconsciously adapted by the partnership, which soon started referring to it as the E.C.

Compensation was a more difficult issue. No less than the partners' opulent lifestyles were at stake. Conceivably, if the profits were doled out inequitably, the ease with which Carolyn Clark made her mortgage on her East Hampton getaway, Worenklein decorated his rambling Englewood, New Jersey, home, and Immergut went on fishing expeditions in the Azores would be hampered.

The floor debate ricocheted between emotional, philosophical, and economic issues. At times, the discussion seemed to be going nowhere. By moving partners up and down the salary scale, the firm's management would be able to reward partners who worked harder, and warn those who were unwilling or unable to keep up with the high standards Milbank had set for its lawyers. Although there was no point to merit compensation if productive partners were not rewarded and their unproductive counterparts not penalized, much time was devoted to an argument over whether compensation should be used as a management tool. Money, argued some, doesn't motivate the partners of Milbank, Tweed. The bulk of the partners, however, were not so naïve. Only about 35 percent of the partnership ended up voting that compensation should not be used as a management tool.

Forger polled the partnership on whether they wanted lockstep to continue to be the basis of their compensation system. Almost everyone in the room, including Worenklein, voted in the affirmative. Though the partners expressed their fears that the compensation committee would attach too high a premium to new business and billable hours, a motion that a partner's pay could not deviate more than 10 percent from that of the rest of his classmates was rejected. To partners on both ends of the political spectrum it seemed dangerous to bog down the compensation committee with too-stringent criteria. The plan's flexibility was a comfort to many and was one reason it got widespread support. The partners announced that they trusted their partners implicitly; whoever was designated to do the job already had their confidence.

At the end of the afternoon, Forger took a final vote. He asked the partners to indicate their support for the proposal and a flood of hands went up. When he asked to see the hands of the dissenters, not one was raised. "It was a rousing end to a very exhaustive session," Forger said.

In less than forty-eight hours, Milbank had been reshaped. The retreat was a landmark in the firm's 120-year history. The firm committee had been replaced and lockstep had been modified. The overwhelming surge of approval for the new plan didn't signify total support. Larry Nelson had not had a dramatic change of heart.

It was simply that, in the Milbank tradition, the partners opposed to the plan realized they had lost, and joined the consensus. Their affirmative vote signified their loyalty to and confidence in their partners. They would do their best to embrace the merit-compensation plan as if it were their own. "There was a sufficient groundswell for change," explained Jerome, who would have preferred to stick with lockstep. "If you didn't listen to it, [it] could affect collegiality. . . . Now I will devote my all to not saying no, but making sure it works."

The partners were free to go home. Many felt they had reached some sort of epiphany. True, they had agonized over this for years, but they had reached a resolution. "People were really euphoric," remembered one partner.

Worenklein was more confident than ever that Milbank could rebound, attract fresh outside talent, and retake its place alongside the other legal superpowers. "We will get some people from other firms that will shock people," he bragged shortly after the retreat.

In a sense the victory belonged to Alex Forger. Cullis had argued and Worenklein had agitated for change, and they deserved much of the credit for pulling their partners away from their ancient ways—but the partners of Milbank, Tweed could never have been persuaded by an outsider like Cullis, or a radical like Worenklein. Forger had taken it slowly—albeit too slowly for the tastes of some. Talking to the Milbankers in their own language, showing them that they did not have to abandon their traditions completely, he had used their beloved consensus-building to lure them into the modern age.

For Forger, the retreat marked the end of a period of frustration. His partners gave him a lot of credit for pulling off the retreat so smoothly. Even Hackett, whose sympathies were with Nelson, thought that Forger had done a "masterful job." His gentle approach, Jerome said, had been perfect for the retreat. "Forger, I have to say, orchestrated this thing beautifully," he said.

The progressive partners felt that, finally, the partnership was ready to implement change. "It took us fifteen months to take a baby step," said Lilley, who had long ago urged his partners to adjust to the new economic realities. Only after the retreat, he said, did "I have confidence that this organization is now capable of not only survival but articulating objectives and planning to meet objectives."

Milbank's first step toward implementing its new strategy was the election of the new executive and compensation committees on April 3. It was deemed such an important event that Ed Reilly asked the judge in the Johnson trial to break early so he could be there to vote for his friend Alex Forger.

The election took place in Conference Room 48D, the Venezuela Room, which had been set up with additional chairs to accommodate the partnership. Aside from the Chase auditorium many floors below, it was the only available conference room big enough to hold all the partners. The proceedings took on a tinge of

Academy Awards–style grandiosity. Two auditors from Price Waterhouse, Milbank's regular accounting firm, had been enlisted to count votes. The job could easily have been handled by Milbank's administrative staff.

The rules for this event were drawn up by Worenklein and litigator Russell Brooks, one of the newest members of the soon-to-be-defunct firm committee. It was to be an open, one-partner one-vote election; any partner who garnered a specific percentage of the vote was automatically put on the executive or compensation committee. There would then be a run-off between the other top contenders. Telephone contact was established between One Chase Manhattan Plaza and partners in Hong Kong, Singapore, Tokyo, and London.

Since he was so obviously a candidate himself, it was deemed inappropriate for Forger to report on the election results. William Jackson, his predecessor, was installed as Milbank's anchorman; he was armed with a blackboard instead of electronic tote boards. Each partner wrote down the name of his or her candidate for chairman of the executive committee on a blank sheet of paper and put it into an envelope. Those in foreign offices were polled over the phone lines. After the Price Waterhouse auditors counted the votes, Jackson announced that Alex Forger was elected chairman, with roughly 80 percent of the vote. His victory was no surprise to the lawyers he had led through the retreat. He strode to the front of the room and replaced Jackson as monitor.

Before the elections, Worenklein had predicted that

either he or Puleo would be elected to the executive committee, but not both. It was unlikely that the partnership would want two young leaders on the committee. For partners who were nervous about Milbank's new direction, Puleo was easier to vote for. He was far more low-key and cautious than Worenklein. While Cullis talked of Worenklein's "perceived rashness," he called Puleo "highly respected for his reasoned positions." Personally, Puleo could be inscrutable, almost cold. But his rationality seemed far less intimidating than Worenklein's radicalism.

Also in Puleo's favor was his strong relationship with Chase; some partners still felt it appropriate that Chase's needs be a significant concern of the management of the firm. On the other hand, some partners thought that Worenklein should devote his energies to rainmaking and his practice. Putting Worenklein, who billed 3,000 hours a year, on the committee would be a loss to the firm, they believed.

More ballots were distributed, marked, and collected. Partners milled about drinking coffee and chatting about client business as the Price Waterhouse people tallied up the vote. When the auditors were finished, Forger announced the results. Floyd Brandow, already a member of the firm committee, had won enough votes to take a seat on the new executive committee. As caretaker of the New York Stock Exchange, one of the firm's most significant corporate clients, Brandow had proved his mettle. He had rotated in and out of Milbank's governance for years. In Cullis's words,

Brandow was "mainstream" and "wise." Back in 1984, Brandow had supported the addition of a merit component to the lockstep plan. But he had questioned the wisdom of Worenklein's proposal that the firm open a Los Angeles office. He had the respect of the firm's conservatives as well as its liberals.

Worenklein was out of the running. Both he and Al Lilley had received a healthy number of votes, but not enough to make it into a run-off. There were now two contenders for the third slot on the executive committee: Puleo and Frank Logan.

The two Chase powers were pitted against one another. When the votes were again counted, Puleo had pulled ahead of his mentor. It was clear that the partners wanted a young representative on the committee. There was also much sentiment that Logan—who routinely put in seventy-hour weeks—had too much on his plate. "It would have been unfair," said trusts-and-estates partner Sam Polk. "It would not have been an intelligent allocation of resources."

It was time to move on to the election of the two partners who, with members of the executive committee, would form the compensation committee. This was a more ticklish selection. The compensation committee would be making subjective decisions, and there was plenty of room for interpretation in the intentionally vague guidelines that would govern their evaluation of partners. Their mandate was to keep lockstep as the basis of the system, but what exactly did that mean? As tax partner Burt Abrams put it, "One man's idea of tinkering is not necessarily going to be another man's idea of tinkering." The five partners would determine whether Milbank's egalitarian character remained intact or whether, as Nelson feared, "only the workaholics will survive and flourish."

The partners decided it was safest to go with the firm's moderates; they elected Sam Polk. Trusts-and-estates partners had traditionally played an important role in Milbank's management; these lawyers had to be able to finesse the personal and economic needs of individuals. Polk was not a political activist, but as chairman of the legal personnel committee, which oversaw associate compensation and evaluation, he had experience navigating sticky personnel problems. He also had time to devote to management. The pace of his practice, serving Chase's trust department and members of the Getty family, was busy but not frenzied.

The final run-off was between trusts-and-estates partner William Crandall, whose clients included members of the "Cousins" generation of the Rockefeller family, and banking partner Joe Siphron. Siphron, a former member of the legal personnel committee, won.

Polk and Siphron were perceived as decent and well liked by the partnership. One partner called the compensation committee "as sensitive a group of partners as you can imagine."

The election was over at about nine o'clock. It had taken two hours, and at least one partner was surprised that it had gone so easily. The winners were congratulated. "It was sort of an unusual situation because we had never had an election before," said Polk. "I felt it was a tribute in a way, and I felt I had an obligation." The partners abroad went to work or to sleep, depending upon what continent they lived on, and their counterparts at One Chase headed home or back to their offices.

Frank Puleo got into his car and headed to Maryland, where he had business to attend to the next day. During the roughly three-hour drive south he pondered his new responsibilities. He had known that his election was a possibility, yet he had mixed feelings about it. Ever since he had been chosen to go on the firm committee, he had devoted a considerable amount of time to management; the streamlined E.C. would demand at least a third of his time. It was a hefty commitment that would eat into his practice. Nevertheless, he couldn't help being flattered—and happy. Two years after Forger's election, Milbank finally had up-to-date management and compensation muscle. Puleo had been given the opportunity to help make both work.

9

THE
DEATH OF
COLLEGIALITY

THE MEMBERS OF MIL-
bank's new compensation committee started meeting
shortly after the election. The partners on the committee
liked to talk about their responsibilities in utopian terms.
Siphron said the committee's "primary function [was] to
encourage and support" partners and their work. "The
objective," echoed Forger, "is to help partners achieve
their maximum potential."

As usual, the Milbank partners were putting a rosy
spin on some serious, and potentially painful, business.

Although some partners may have swallowed the sugar-coated explanations, the bottom line was that the committee was taking money away from some partners and giving it to others. The committee was punishing dead weight. And they were trying to keep the firm's stars from being cherry-picked.

As the five partners charged with determining the financial future of their peers worked in secrecy, they continued to maintain that the "core" of lockstep would remain intact. Seemingly there were limitations on how far they could go. The partnership had made it clear they wanted no "tinkering" with a given partner's compensation based on a single extraordinary or catastrophic year. "The norm is a high standard," Polk said. But at the spring retreat the partnership had given the compensation committee a broad mandate. The reality was that the five partners could define the "norm" and the "core" of lockstep any way they pleased.

The committee's plan of attack was to visit every partner and talk about his or her practice and the performance of other partners in the firm. It had been decided that Joe Siphron and Sam Polk, the two members of the committee who were not also on the executive committee, would conduct the interviews because they had more time. Siphron and Polk divided up the list of partners and started on a door-to-door tour of the firm. The two lawyers stayed in constant touch with each other, seeking points of agreement. Soon after they started making their rounds, a consensus emerged. On quite a few of their early forays, they were told by colleagues that Forger deserved to be lifted above the top class—called the piano class by some because the large class was held up by the legs of the partnership.

This was to spark the committee's only major disagreement. When the partners convened in June, Forger suggested that members of the committee not be eligible for raises beyond those routinely given to members of their class. That one of the five members might be cut was a nonissue. The partnership would never have elected a poor performer. All five were solid citizens.

"Joe and I reported that it was a clear consensus that [Forger] should be elevated," Polk recalled. Nevertheless Forger was adamant. He felt it would create a bad appearance for compensation-committee members to elevate themselves, especially in the first year when credibility really counted. Brandow, Puleo, Polk, and Siphron all tried to dissuade Forger, but he was immovable. "We finally ceded to his wishes," said Polk.

Forger's hefty partnership draw of roughly $500,000 still didn't make the extra $75,000 or so he was passing up negligible. Unlike some of his partners, his income from the firm was not supplemented by independent wealth. Forger's leadership act was a bit overpowering at times, but few, if anyone, at Milbank doubted his sincerity. His financial sacrifice proved once again that he was a true patriot.

Painfully aware that they all had a lot to lose, or gain, the Milbank partners prepared carefully for their meetings with Siphron and Polk. They struggled over the "statements" the committee had requested. What was to be addressed in the statement was left vague. Siphron described it as a summary of how each partner "views his professional life—a base from which to start discussions, a running start for the interview."

Most interviews lasted an hour or so, although a few ran much longer. It turned out that many partners did have some sort of personal business plan. They talked about their objectives for the coming year, and how the firm could help support their efforts. Business generation was almost always a point of discussion.

Even partners who had little to fear from the interrogators felt awkward. "You feel kind of weird talking about yourself and your practice," said Alan W. Kornberg, a protégé of John Jerome, who made partner just before the retreat. "You don't often get a chance to take a step back." His classmate Joe Genova found that talking and writing about his practice "makes you feel like you're boasting." Senior partner Roger Oresman, on the other hand, had no such qualms. When Polk dropped by Oresman's office, the senior partner chatted openly about himself and his fellow partners. "I don't have any difficulty talking about anything," he said.

"It was the first venture and it was extremely difficult for four or five people to do," Forger said of the committee's task. "It was time-consuming. We wanted to be fair and comply with due process." The emotional energy the task demanded of the five committeemen could not be attributed solely to the difficult decisions about who would be cut or raised. Many of the weak links had been known for years, and there were some obvious targets for the compensation committee's probe. It was the toll the changes would exact on the affected individuals and the partnership as a whole that made the job so arduous.

The members of the committee hoped that there would be no big surprises. They decided that four out of five members of the committee had to concur on any move up or down the compensation scale. A move of a member of the top class, those who had been partners for fifteen years or more, would require agreement by the full committee. In the end, all five members agreed on every decision. "There was no advocacy, no debate," Forger said. "It just seemed to fall pretty naturally."

For most partners, the immediacy of the switch from lockstep had worn off. The intervening months had given them other things to worry about: client business, evaluating senior associates for partnership, and Worenklein's Los Angeles proposal, which was nearing a partnership vote. Shortly before the meeting to announce the changes, however, rumors about who would be affected had begun to circulate despite the committee's attempt to impose a news blackout. Real estate partner Hackett had heard some of the gossip around a lunch table just before the meeting.

On a late afternoon in October, the partners of Milbank, Tweed filed into the Venezuela Room to hear the six-month-old compensation committee issue its first report. Finally, the partners would learn who would get a boost in compensation, who would stay on the lockstep level, and who would face the humiliation of a pay cut. Forger, Brandow, Puleo, Polk, and Siphron took seats at the front of the room. As usual, Forger acted as master of ceremonies.

When all the partners were seated, Forger began to recite the results of the committee's work. He told his partners that the committee had rewarded the super-human efforts of three partners already in the top compensation class. Frank Logan had devoted his life to tending the Chase relationship; John Jerome had made a name for himself in the bankruptcy world and built a burgeoning practice at Milbank; and Al Lilley had launched his own corporate group with an independent clientele, all the while serving the needs of the Rockefeller family. The three would now comprise a new class of partners above their peers.

The committee had also elevated three midlevel partners, Forger announced. Not surprisingly, Jay Worenklein was rewarded for his rainmaking, his efforts to thrust the firm into the investment-banking and utilities arenas, and his never-ending fight to push Milbank, Tweed toward the next century. Elliot Gewirtz was recognized for his flourishing Japanese practice, and Warren Cooke was elevated in recognition of his nearly nine years in exile building the Hong Kong end of the Pacific Basin business.

Forger also had some less pleasant news. Eight partners had received warnings that if their productivity did not pick up during the next six months, they would either not get raises with the rest of their class or they would get a pay cut. The six-month lag was a built-in due-process protection mechanism that had been discussed at the retreat. In order to spare these lawyers embarrassment, they were not named in front of the crowd in Conference Room 48D. But Forger assured the assembled partners that the affected lawyers had been told of their predicament.

Finally, Forger dropped what could only have been described as a bombshell: Two of the eight partners would be leaving the firm. Forger did name these two partners: Jeffrey Tallackson, a banking partner, and Norman R. Nelson, a litigator, both of whom had made partner in 1979 and should have been in the prime of their careers. Both were known as lackluster business producers. The chairman insisted that he and his fellow committee members had not out-and-out fired Tallackson and Nelson. But it appeared to many of the partners in 48D that evaluations of the two partners had been handled in such a way that the gentlemen had no other logical—or dignified—recourse but to decide to withdraw from the partnership.

Those partners who turned to look at the expressions on Tallackson and Nelson's faces in their moment of supreme humiliation were disappointed. The two had been warned by the committee, and neither had showed up for the meeting.

The committee's work, Forger continued, was not yet finished. On January 1, seven more partners would be elevated. Some had already been informed of their impending raises, but the committee was not yet prepared to reveal their names. For the time being, he added, there would be no further bad news.

When Forger concluded his announcement there was very little discussion. The partners were stunned. Often they had talked about a "handful" of projected deviations from the lockstep path. "You raise a hand and you see five," trusts-and-estates partner Crandall said. "I think we all interpreted 'handful' literally."

Charles Peet, the banking partner who had launched the London office, was one of the few partners who did speak up. "I said that according to my calculations, my rough calculations, approximately a third of the partners were going to be moved up or down and that I had been under the impression that the substantial majority of the partners were going to remain on lockstep," Peet recalled. He felt the committee had acted "very aggressively."

Forger responded that because the committee thought it best not to step into the plan gingerly, it had attempted to redress inequities that had long existed in the firm's pay structure. In the future, he said, the partners could expect to see far fewer changes in any given year.

Because they'd done little to prepare the full partnership for the dramatic change, the compensation committee was somewhat to blame for the partners' shock. Over the previous months they had underplayed their role, couching their mandate in glossy, hopeful terms. The cuts stung more than they would have had the committee provided prior hints of the extent of their pruning.

The compensation committee was the crack through which the real world, where partners were expected to produce or pay a price for their inactivity, seeped into and ate away at the firm's rarefied atmosphere. Its nineteenth-century milieu was gone forever.

During its investigation, the committee had found proof that all partners were not equal—that contributions to the firm's profitability varied tremendously. When faced with the evidence, committee members had felt they had no choice but to take drastic action.

The litigation department, where business had fallen off, was an obvious target. The growth of the in-house litigation capability at Chase and the scarcity of large cases meant that short of a miracle or an expensive lateral hire the department was not apt to see an upturn in business soon. The partners could depend on Reilly, Richard Tufaro, and Russell Brooks to run whatever complex cases came along. They had high hopes that the youngest partners' talent would some day attract business. But there were midlevel partners who were deemed less capable of running or attracting large matters and who were rarely turned to for assistance by their partners. At least two litigators, who had been admitted to the partnership during the department's heyday, and had once played important but secondary roles in cases run by senior partners, seemed to have lost their bearings.

Norman Nelson, forty, one of the partners encouraged to leave the firm, was a rather withdrawn young partner proficient at the analysis of complex material in very large cases. As a senior associate in the late 1970s, he had been assigned to a very large breach-of-contract suit filed by Armco Inc. against Allied Chemical Corporation, represented by Bill Jackson. That, explained a lawyer who was Nelson's fellow associate at the time, helped take him through partnership because it would have been impractical to pass over an associate immersed in an important case on the eve of trial. Milbank lost the case in 1980 and the firm's client settled for $20 million. By the time Nelson finished up his work on the matter, the firm, along with many others on Wall Street, had entered a litigation slump, due in part to the slowdown in antitrust work during the Reagan administration. "Business slackened off and he wasn't having work assigned to him," said the former fellow associate. "In the end he didn't carry his weight."

The compensation committee, after quizzing the litigation partners and conducting careful interviews with Nelson, resolved that the partnership might be healthier without him. According to a partner, when compensation committee members discussed their evaluation of Nelson with other partners, Reilly offered to split his compensation between Nelson and another lawyer who was warned by the committee.

When the compensation committee members turned their attention to the banking department they saw that Jeffrey Tallackson, more than any other partner, was operating without a safety net. In a sense he was a victim of the growing might of Chase's in-house legal department. Although the percentage of Milbank's revenues attributable to their favorite client had diminished, the amount of work had continued to rise, albeit at an ever slower rate. For the most part, the banking partners remained busy, and every year they were able to justify the making of more partners.

But Tallackson had always been an oddity in the department because of his specialty in consumer-banking work. Chase's decision to take consumer-credit work in-house had left Tallackson with less to do. "He really didn't have any power base in the banking department. Jeff was really being thrown the dregs of work," said a Milbank lawyer. There was grumbling that Tallackson wasn't working very hard. Even the more insular Milbank partners had become alert to the necessity of leveraging, or delegating work to junior lawyers, and Tallackson was not keeping associates very busy.

Before the announcement, a compensation-committee member paid banking partner Charles Peet a call because he had worked with Tallackson in the past. When Peet was told that Tallackson would be encouraged to leave, he didn't argue the point. He had not been overly impressed with Haberkern's argument in 1978 that Tallackson should be made a partner. "I thought the case was misguided and wrong and I think that's proven to be the case," he said bluntly.

The compensation committee had turned up little to sway them from their decision. Tallackson did not generate significant business; few of his colleagues stood behind him. In short, he was doomed.

The committee had decided to tell individual partners they would be shifted off the lockstep track before they made the announcement to the full partnership. Not surprisingly, there was a wide range of reaction to the news. The elevation of the three senior partners had been one of the committee's easiest judgments. Accordingly two of those giants, Logan and Jerome, were not surprised to learn that they would be rewarded for their contribution to the firm. The third, Al Lilley, was more taken aback. Siphron recalled that one of the six partners raised exclaimed: "I don't feel I'm any more deserving than twenty other partners." Siphron was heartened by that reaction. "It demonstrates how much we value teamwork and stay away from focusing on individual efforts," he said.

In order to emphasize the significance of the message, at least two partners on the committee went to every meeting at which a partner was encouraged to leave or told his pay might be cut. "They are very difficult discussions," said Siphron. While the rewarded partners each received about $75,000 in additional compensation, their less fortunate colleagues could expect to see their income drop by about $100,000.

When confronted, most of these partners told the committee that they had not been aware of the problem. "I've been here twenty years, why didn't somebody tell me?" asked one unhappy partner. Forger, noting this refrain, saw a shortcoming of the partnership as a whole:

"a failure of the partners in great numbers to be candid in discussing weaknesses." It was not surprising in a firm where saving face and avoiding hurt feelings was not only a priority but a tradition.

The committee's news to Tallackson and Nelson was worded very carefully. There was a built-in mechanism for saving face in the committee's message. "Nobody was asked to leave literally," explained a member of the compensation committee. Instead the two partners were simply told, "We are likely going to be recommending that you withdraw," this committee member explained.

Tallackson found his partners' rejection so offensive that he soon after walked out and never returned to his office again, although he periodically used Milbank's uptown office. Many of his assignments were passed off to other lawyers. Associates were told nothing about his disappearance. Banking associates joked that he had "vaporized."

The circumspect manner in which the bad news was delivered at least protected Nelson and Tallackson from ridicule from outside the firm. "The outside world only knows that he's a bright guy," said a compensation-committee member about Nelson.

Tallackson and Nelson declined to discuss their departures from the firm. Tallackson became executive vice president, general counsel, and secretary at the American Savings Bank. Nelson became general counsel at the New York Clearinghouse Association.

In the weeks following Forger's announcement and Tallackson's exit, the raises, cuts, and impending departures remained a hot topic of discussion among the partners. It took a while for the news to seep in. Some partners who had been skeptical that the firm could dig in and make painful decisions to strengthen itself were heartened by the committee's actions. One partner called it "a first step—not dramatic." Said bankruptcy partner Barry Radick shortly after the meeting: "It's a tribute to Forger and his little band of merry men." Hackett, who had supported the position of his mentor, Larry Nelson, congratulated Gewirtz and sent Worenklein a note. "I was tickled for him and delighted," he said. He could afford to be gracious. In his feedback session with the committee he had been informed that he would be among those elevated on January 1. Institutional-finance expert Mel Immergut and litigator Richard Tufaro would be in this group as well.

For some partners, however, the shock was turning to anger. "Most people didn't expect them to be as decisive as they were," remarked a pro-change partner. Forger admitted that there was "some disbelief" and that it was "traumatic." But those assessments of the partnership's mood seriously underplayed the emotion and tension that continued to build that fall and early winter. Even partners who were not activists were upset. In the past, when profits were divvied up at the end of the year, lockstep had guarded against bruised feelings. The partners had known they were forfeiting a safeguard when they adopted merit compensation. But as Peet put it, "We went almost to the other extreme, [the] opposite end of the spectrum.

"In my judgment they acted too aggressively in a situation where we had virtually no experience at all," he said. "They took some steps and followed some procedures that I think, I won't say a majority of the firm, but a substantial number of people in the firm, felt were not the best way to proceed."

Finally, in December, Larry Nelson blew the issue into the open. He circulated a memo to the partnership, a response to the compensation committee's announcement. His memo was sent to partners in a manila envelope marked "Private and Confidential" with a seal over the flap—the kind of envelope that even the most trusted secretaries did not open. Once again, Nelson was on the warpath. For most Milbank lawyers, December meant not New Year's Eve parties, but sleepless nights finishing up deals that had to be closed before the end of the year. Nelson, however, had found time for some serious thinking.

He was, of course, unhappy about the changes. His speech at the March retreat was one of the best-remembered moments in the firm's two-year debate on this delicate issue. The memo was short and to the point. Too many partners had been taken off the lockstep scale, he argued. The five partners on the compensation committee had gone way beyond their mandate. Mechanisms for greater due process had to be incorporated to protect the partnership.

It went against Milbank tradition that Nelson, in his very effort to preserve the firm's traditions, should try to incite a rebellion of sorts by distributing a provocative memo. If Nelson had wanted to adhere to Milbank custom, he would have joined the majority to support the compensation committee and make the system work, no matter how repugnant he found it personally. There were several schools of thought about why Nelson was unable to let the matter drop. "It's more psychological than anything else," explained an older partner. "He hates to see change occur." Cullis, who had left his post as executive director and become a law-firm management consultant, had always found Nelson difficult to deal with. He thought that Nelson overidentified with the institution: "He thinks of Milbank as one of the very finest things that ever happened to him."

Nelson, however, was hardly alone in his misgivings. In fact, quite a few partners felt uneasy and angry precisely for the reasons Nelson spelled out in his memo. "I tend to agree with Larry that this went a little too far," said Peter Herman, the partner who oversaw David Rockefeller's real estate work. Like Nelson, Herman was dismayed at the number of lawyers affected. But he was especially upset that Forger had given the partnership only a sketchy explanation about why two partners were encouraged to leave. Forger's insistence that the committee wanted to avoid embarrassing the partners didn't make Herman feel any better. "There's never been a public explanation about why those folks should leave," he complained. "If I can't compare their situation to mine or any other partner's situation, it leaves me very uneasy as a partner. Unless the story comes out one will not know where they stand."

Forger sensed that Nelson's position was gaining support in the partnership. Although it was rare for a partnership meeting to be called to discuss a single issue, Forger knew that he had to do something to quell the unrest among the firm's conservatives. A meeting was scheduled for January 7, giving partners just enough time to recover from their year-end deals or winter holidays. The seven additional partner raises the compensation committee had promised on January 1 were put on hold until after the dissent could be sorted out at the meeting.

Forger's strategy for running the January meeting was typical of the unique Milbank style. It would have been easy to rally a show of strength; had Forger requested their assistance, Worenklein, Oresman, or any member of the compensation committee would likely have been pleased to prepare rousing speeches supporting the committee's actions. Instead, Forger planned to let unhappy partners have their say and put his committee on the defensive. To deny Nelson and his cohorts the opportunity to voice their concerns would have alienated partners from both ends of the political spectrum.

As he had at the retreat almost a year before, Forger yielded the floor to Nelson. The senior real estate partner argued that the compensation committee had gone well beyond its mandate by lifting or lowering so many partners off the lockstep track and making it impossible for Nelson and Tallackson to remain partners. He then reiterated the themes he had hammered at previously:

the potential for divisiveness between partners, and the lack of cooperation that merit compensation could breed in client work.

Michael F. Orr, a banking partner for over twenty years, then made his pitch. Quite a few partners, he said, were unhappy that their colleagues deemed serious underperformers by the compensation committee had not had adequate opportunity to hear the criticisms lodged against them and defend themselves. Orr lamented the lack of safeguards against unjust or misguided judgments by the committee.

Partner Charles Peet then took the floor. It was not like him to involve himself in this kind of intra-firm dispute: the last time he had taken a vocal position on anything management-related was when he and other partners had convinced the partnership to open a London office. Usually Peet kept his mouth shut and devoted himself to bank work in his silent, white corner office on the forty-eighth floor.

Peet didn't have strong feelings one way or the other about lockstep and merit compensation, but he felt he had to take a stand. He feared that the scaled-down executive committee was not hearing the full range of complaints from the partnership. He focused his remarks on the way the five members of the compensation committee had gone about collecting and interpreting the information on which they based their decisions. "In my judgment the compensation committee took less care in the partnership appraisal process than we do in the associate appraisal process and I don't think that's appropriate," Peet said. He felt the committee took too casual an approach and that it may have relied on flawed data.

After Peet finished speaking, Forger took control of the meeting. He stood before his partners and called for a vote. Who still supported the new compensation system as put into effect by the committee, he asked his partners? A forest of hands went up in support. Nelson's revolt had quickly been turned into a temper tantrum. Ultimately he lost because the bulk of his partners were convinced that following the example of their more aggressive competitors was worth the sacrifice.

There were other reasons for Nelson's failure. After all, his bid was not a guaranteed loser—two years before he would have had every partner in the firm behind him. Nelson was a rabble-rouser, and an effective one, but his potential sources of support were wedded to Milbank's tradition of acquiescence. They were for the most part a conservative lot, not the types to jump on a bandwagon headed against the management of the firm. "We don't have time to go around and join forces usually," said Peet.

These were lawyers' lawyers. Orr, a senior banking partner, was steeped in the firm's traditions. Like Peet, he had devoted much of his life to Chase. Peter Herman was a jovial, energetic young lawyer, but he was not a leader. Reilly, who also preferred the old Milbank to the new, could not be counted upon to champion a cause that went against the wishes of his dearest friend within the firm, Alex Forger. These stalwarts had been brought up to believe that the firm's ultimate source of strength, in the past and the future, was consensus. They didn't have the stomach—or perhaps the political know-how—to turn the tide in their direction. They were not bred for revolution.

The fact that Milbank's men happened to be lawyers also played a role in their complacency. A lawyer is taught to trust hard evidence. His work is guided by documentation. This is especially true for banking lawyers who spend days, often weeks, preparing lengthy loan agreements. Conjecture carries little weight with them. Therefore one of the chief complaints about the compensation committee—that it had provided little explanation for why and how it made its decisions—also served as a brake on some of the partners' inclinations to question or challenge the outcome of the deliberations. "I think that it's very difficult to second-guess the compensation committee when you don't have the same facts they do," said Oresman. "It doesn't make sense to second-guess them."

Partner George J. Forsyth, whose quiet toil in the corporate department was confined largely to certain portions of the securities laws, thought the committee had overstepped its bounds. He also believed, though, that he had forfeited his right to challenge the committee when he designated its members to act as his representatives. "I have to respect their judgment [because] I was not a party to their judgment," he said. The five partners elected to divvy up the profits, Forsyth added, were "men of principle, men of fairness and good judgment. Once you opt for that process you really take the results with that in mind. . . . It's like a jury acquitting somebody if you weren't in the room. The process is at work. We convict a lot of innocent people each year, but the process is there. It's not going to work perfectly."

At other firms, disputes over compensation often led to defections and spinoffs of groups of partners. But because Milbank had an institutional practice, most of the conservative partners couldn't exercise the option to "vote with their feet," as Finley, Kumble's Marshall Manley was fond of saying. They didn't have enough economic clout to threaten to leave if they didn't get their way. Nelson had what is usually referred to as "portable business"—a clientele that would follow him wherever he went—but many other valuable and productive partners couldn't count on moving their business. Orr and Peet weren't going to lure the Chase Manhattan Bank from Milbank. Whether Herman could take his portion of the eldest Rockefeller brother's work with him was entirely open to question.

It is, of course, unlikely that these partners even considered leaving the firm. They were born and bred Milbankers. Both financially and emotionally they were incapable of jumping ship, even if the ship had changed its course.

The management revolution at Milbank, Tweed was complete. There would be more skirmishes, but the forward-looking partners had won. Milbank was finally freed from the constraints of an archaic governance that assumed that all partners were equal. Now growth and diversification could be more than "buzzwords." The firm could compete with its peer firms for new talent. It could move more quickly to identify and snap up senior lawyers. Rainmakers could be offered large sums of money, regardless of how long ago they graduated from law school—and Milbank could provide incentives to its homegrown stars as well.

A high price had been paid for entry into this new world, however. Never was that more evident than in the final days of 1986 and early 1987 when roughly twenty partners had either benefited or suffered from the modification of lockstep. There were plenty of bruised egos walking the halls of One Chase Manhattan Plaza that winter. In a sense, Larry Nelson's predictions were coming true. "There's no question that the firm has become more competitive, more aggressive, and less collegial than it was fifteen years ago," said Immergut, a beneficiary of the second wave of raises. Nevertheless, he still thought the firm was more collegial than most. Forger added: "It's no longer as satisfying or pleasing or comfortable—the word is collegial. It is surely not as collegial as it was in the old days."

The younger lawyers were prepared to make that sacrifice—but for many of the older lawyers, it seemed as though the executive committee, egged on by young aggressive partners, would not be content until they had dismantled every remnant of the old Milbank.

By 1987, Forger thought the gratifying parts of his

job were long overdue. For the first time, he saw that he had made real progress in moving the firm forward. He could now predict that "ten years from now we will be quite a different firm. We will be as good or better a firm as we are today." Still, Forger found the job to be relatively joyless and he felt very much alone. "I don't have a close group of contemporaries," he complained shortly after the January meeting. "I just happen to be the oldest one alive." He had alienated the few partners in his age group—Larry Nelson, Reilly, former managing partner Francis Musselman, and trusts-and-estates partner Carroll Wainwright, he said. "All in one way or another liked the way the firm was before."

Forger saw a schism between his contemporaries and their younger partners. The elder partners, he explained, "seem to have been more affected by the transition. That is the body that requires most attention, and the younger element has to understand that there was life before present times." It was that aspect of his job, placating the partners who looked back with nostalgia at a professional life that could no longer survive, that Forger found the most "trying" and the "most disconcerting."

"I am not enjoying the job," he said shortly after the initial shocks of merit compensation had begun to fade. "A lot of people would think it's a pretty heady experience to have the position. [But] there is no sense of power. The power is only in persuasion and recommending and I would not want it otherwise. . . . It ain't Miller time."

10

THE
LATERAL
INVASION

THE COMPENSATION
committee's decisions continued to eat away at Ed Reilly.
Even after the two departing partners found jobs Reilly
continued to fume. He was moved by the grace with
which another partner who had received an extreme
admonishment quietly withdrew from the partnership,
but his strong sense of loyalty was offended. He saw the
departures as "the antithesis" of partnership, he said. "I
don't think the people in the firm realized what a devastating blow they were dealing." Reilly, who was di-

vorced, called it "worse than a marital split," and briefly considered leaving the firm himself.

As Milbank pursued its growth-and-diversification strategy, the firm seemed less and less like the firm Reilly had grown up with. Years before, he had warned Worenklein that Milbank was a gem, to be valued and preserved. That gem had been recut, and Reilly had problems with the results. "We call ourselves a partnership but we're becoming much more like a corporation," he said bitterly.

He found the events of late 1986 and of 1987 particularly troublesome. Milbank's campaign to transform itself continued to batter the litigation department. And Reilly's pride was hurt as younger and more progressive partners challenged his leadership and philosophy about what Milbank ought to be.

It was an odd time for Reilly to be feeling so poorly about his career at Milbank. In June 1986, on behalf of the children of Johnson & Johnson heir J. Seward Johnson, he had trounced Sullivan & Cromwell and its client, the children's stepmother, in the Johnson estate case. In the children's fight against what had appeared to be an ironclad will, Reilly had argued that Seward had been too elderly and infirm to make intelligent decisions about disposing his approximately $400 million fortune. His wife Basia and Shearman & Sterling associate Nina S. Zagat had exerted "undue influence" on the fragile old man, Reilly told a transfixed courtroom. Reilly's dramatic rendition of the family's tale had wowed the jury and judge and wrestled Basia, Zagat, and their trial counsel, Sullivan & Cromwell, into such an untenable position that they decided to settle the case and pay the children between $125 and $150 million. Milbank's $10 million fee included a premium of approximately $1 million added by Forger, who was largely responsible for negotiating the settlement.

Reilly had been devastated that the jury would never decide his case. He had convinced himself that the will contest's significance went way beyond a skirmish between rich people; he thought that a favorable verdict would create new law to protect the infirm from undue influence when making their wills. After the settlement his partners thought he seemed listless. The departure of some of his partners only seemed to increase his sense of loss.

In fact, Reilly had accomplished something that many members of New York's legal community would have thought nearly impossible. He had focused the world's attention on Milbank's litigation expertise, and the department threatened to emerge from near-oblivion. Reilly's courtroom prowess had been displayed in all of New York's daily newspapers and several national magazines. His victory over high-profile litigators at Sullivan & Cromwell was noticed by lawyers who had almost forgotten that Milbank even had a litigation department. Even some of Reilly's partners were awed by his success. Reilly's protégé, Charles Berry, had sent copies of his powerful opening statement all over the firm. One lawyer even read it to his children at bedtime. Other partners stole time away from their practices to get a glimpse of Reilly's trial performance.

As the glory wore off, however, Milbank's litigation

partners realized that the excitement Reilly had breathed into the department would wane along with the press reports of the trial. A will contest didn't do much to boost the reputation of a financial-services law firm like Milbank. Reilly's success was not likely to bring in the kind of big-ticket corporate litigation that Cravath, Skadden, and other firms were routinely hired to handle. Several litigation partners, especially Richard Tufaro, brooded about the litigation department's future. Tufaro was known throughout the firm as an extremely hard worker and a talented technician. He was also a skeptic, acutely aware of his department's shortcomings.

There was good reason to worry. When Charles Berry and Joe Genova became litigation partners in 1986, their elevations marked the department's first associate promotions in five years. As a result of the growth of an in-house litigation group at Chase, the department had lost work it had once taken for granted. Once, Milbank had overseen Chase's litigation all over the globe. By 1986, in-house lawyers not only supervised Milbank and other law firms, but handled litigation as well. Only roughly 10 percent of the litigation department's work came from Chase. During William Jackson's heyday, cases from the stock exchange had been plentiful, but most of the exchange's litigation problems had since almost dried up. Among associates there were rumors that Milbank would abolish the department altogether.

Milbank's litigators weren't languishing, but the department was static in size and wasn't contributing significantly to the firm's profitability. Tufaro thought that his colleagues needed to develop their rainmaking skills. He also was convinced, however, that to reverse the department's sagging fortunes, the firm needed to bring in a strong, well-known lateral, "somebody," he said, "who was a really fine trial lawyer and somebody who was more in the category of an emerging figure in the New York litigation bar." Years before, of course, the suggestion would have been dismissed by senior partners. But in late 1986 Tufaro had support. After all, the partnership had endorsed change and given the firm's management the tools to make it happen.

Reilly disagreed with Tufaro's assessment of the department's situation, and he much preferred immersing himself in the intricacies of his cases than in the department's woes. "I couldn't persuade him to act, to begin by acknowledging the fact that there is a problem," complained Tufaro. When Tufaro tried to talk to his senior partner about what he felt should be done, Reilly turned to stone. "He wouldn't respond. It was a monologue. He'd say 'Thank you,'" said Tufaro.

Tufaro's frustration reached a high point in late 1986. "Ed won't lead us," he said. "He's killing us."

Reilly had a hands-off attitude toward management. If Tufaro and other partners wanted to bring fresh talent into the department, he told them, they could go ahead and look for it. He reminded them that there were a lot of good lawyers in the department and then let his partners go their own way. He didn't think they would come back with superstars like Arthur L. Liman of Paul, Weiss, Rifkind, Wharton & Garrison or

Robert B. Fiske, Jr., of Davis Polk. "I was very skeptical that we could attract the kind of litigators that everyone was looking for," he said.

So Tufaro and Pete Connick, a litigator who often represented Chase, went hunting. By December, they had found a candidate, and although he was not a major superstar he was close. Sanford M. "Sandy" Litvack was well known in New York and Washington, D.C., legal circles. In 1981, after a two-year stint as assistant attorney general for antitrust, he returned to private practice at Donovan Leisure Newton & Irvine. Shortly thereafter, that prestigious firm faced a major crisis. A victim of the antitrust litigation drought brought on by the Reagan administration's laissez-faire economic policies, the firm began to come apart.

It was Litvack who exercised the leadership necessary to stop the exodus of partners with business. The firm remained intact and its downward slide stopped. By the end of 1986, however, Litvack had tired of his role. Although the firm's fortunes had stabilized, he was unsure that he could restore it to its previous stature. Litvack told his partners that he was leaving, thereby precipitating another crisis, and put himself on the job market.

Litvack's announcement prompted a flood of inquiries from firms needing a litigation boost, including Milbank. It seemed like a good match. Litvack wanted to join a prominent firm that was "not so visible in litigation," he said, "so I could make a difference." He had several other points on his checklist of needs; he wanted to bring two young partners with him from Donovan Leisure, and he wanted to play some management role at his new firm.

Forger badly wanted to bring Litvack to Milbank, and as Christmas 1986 approached he was confident that he and other partners could convince the litigator to join the firm. Nevertheless, in its first foray into the high-stakes competition for talent, Milbank stumbled. Litvack was not an easy man to negotiate with. He did his best to convey what his needs were, but he refused to ask for anything specific. Litvack wanted to be seduced.

Milbank didn't know how to respond. The litigation department was reluctant to invite Litvack's young team along with him. And Forger and other partners were at a loss as to how to give Litvack a management role. They did little more than imply that he would have a role in the running of the litigation department by sheer dint of his personality and experience. Unaddressed was the quandary of how to handle two powerful senior litigators and egos—Litvack and Reilly—in the same department.

Dewey, Ballantine courted Litvack without ambivalence. "I got to know the Dewey people better, faster," he said. After he had a firm offer from Dewey, Litvack spoke to Forger by phone, hoping to get a clearer sense of what Milbank could offer him. Litvack, however, was unable to pin Forger down on what management role he could expect to play in the litigation department. Forger gently chided Litvack, asking him if he wanted Forger's job, or, perhaps, his name added to the firm.

Litvack replied lightly that his name in the firm sounded nice.

Litvack liked Forger. He thought he was honest and even "somewhat inspirational." Forger had a sense of what needed to be done at Milbank, "but he wasn't a bomb-thrower," Litvack said. Nevertheless, he chose Dewey. Litvack wanted to feel wanted, even loved, and Dewey's welcome came without reservations. Litvack joined the firm with his two protégés in January 1987 and took a seat on the firm's management committee.

Milbank's partners accepted Litvack's decision with a mixture of disappointment and relief. Even Tufaro had felt uncomfortable about bringing in Litvack's young partners when young Milbank litigators were clamoring to climb into the partnership. The partners, however, were coming to understand that reconciling collegiality with the firm's new goals would not be easy when decisions had to be made quickly to accommodate partners from the outside.

Shortly after Litvack joined Dewey, Milbank's executive committee overhauled the department chairmanship system. Never again would the issue of leadership be so difficult to resolve. Forger, Puleo, and Brandow thought that stronger management at the departmental level was a must if the firm was to achieve its goals. Traditionally, department chairmen had been the firm's senior practitioners. The new troika solved that problem in early 1987 by simply abolishing the posts. Now, instead of chairmen, there would be departmental administrators. The name change simply helped soften the blow to old-timers and signal that department heads would no longer be able to sit back as though the post were a ceremonial honor. Henceforth they would take a more active role in supervising partners and associates.

For the most part younger men were assigned to the new posts. Of the longtime chairmen, only Frank Logan, in the banking department, made the transition to administrator. Forger relinquished his own departmental responsibilities to William Crandall. Reilly was replaced by Connick and Tufaro.

It fell to Forger to tell Reilly the news. "It could be no other way," said Forger, who hardly looked forward to the task. "Can you imagine," he asked, "going to your best friend? . . ." The chairman worried about how Reilly was weathering the firm's changes. "It may be he doesn't recognize the institution today," Forger said. Forger said he told Reilly that, even though he was being defrocked, "no one could alter the high regard" in which he was held by his partners.

Reilly said he didn't care about the change; he had never liked management, he insisted. As he had prepared for the Johnson trial, administration had become his last priority. During all of 1985 and half of 1986 he had even stopped going to department meetings and abandoned his management responsibilities to Connick and Tufaro. "It was fine with me," he said. "I didn't even know what was going on." When he reclaimed his post after the trial, he had found that he enjoyed it less than ever. He felt that younger partners resented his refusal to embrace change, and he, in turn, resented the new wave of modernism that had overtaken the firm and caused his partners to leave. "What little interest I had in running the department was diminished drastically," he said.

But Tufaro thought that, despite Reilly's protestations to the contrary, he was wounded. "I'm sure in some sense he took it as a rejection. We just fundamentally disagree," said Tufaro shortly after he became co-administrator of the department. "I felt he had to do something. He just couldn't accept that because things had worked in the past they would [necessarily] work in the future."

Tufaro continued sadly: "I've lost a certain amount of warmth I had with him. It's been very difficult. There's a certain amount of hostility."

The new changes in Milbank's management structure also finally helped settle uncertainty that had plagued the tax department for a year. The executive committee troika had aggressively intervened in the department's affairs in mid-1986 to revamp the department.

In recent years, as the partners tried to build the firm's corporate capabilities, they had become concerned about the service they were getting from the tax department. Corporate transactions had become increasingly motivated by complex tax considerations, and partners throughout the firm were worried that the department would not be able to keep up.

For many years Stuart E. Keebler had led the small

group. A partner of the old school, Keebler did his bit to maintain the Chase relationship and handled some Rockefeller family work. Still, he was not a strong leader or manager. Shortly after the executive committee took charge in 1986, he opted for early retirement, and it was widely assumed by partners and associates that he had been encouraged to do so by the firm's new management. Keebler said that he was not encouraged to retire. "I retired very gracefully," he said. "I was the one who wanted to retire early."

Burt Abrams had been next in line to become the department's chairman. His chief qualification was his seniority. Abrams had a retiring personality and a slow work pace. One tax associate who admired his analytical skills and concentration nevertheless conceded that Abrams could "only handle one or two things at once."

Eager to bolster the tax department, the executive committee had started searching for new partners who could generate business and supply the expertise needed for complex deals. Aiding in the effort had been Lilley, who, as a senior corporate partner, had a special interest in bringing in a strong tax presence.

The E.C.'s approach had made partners inside and outside the tax department uncomfortable. Doug Dunn and Milbank's handful of other laterals had been recruited by colleagues in their practice areas. This time the impetus came from outside the department, which was viewed as too weak to take charge of the task. "We were looking for a whole new generation of leadership in that practice area," said a young partner in another department who appreciated the executive committee's efforts.

In May 1986, the executive committee and Lilley had persuaded the partnership to bring in John Colley Baity and L. Anthony Joseph, Jr., of Baity & Joseph. In many ways, Baity and Joseph were the antithesis of what a Milbank partner was supposed to be. The two had moved around a lot. Baity, the senior of the two, had once headed the tax department and been a member of the executive committee of Donovan Leisure. When that firm hit the skids in the early 1980s, in part because of the nationwide decline in antitrust work, he had been one of the early defectors. Despite his fickle past, however, Baity was exactly what Milbank lacked. He was a rainmaker whose clientele included the Walt Disney Company and MCA/Universal City Studios, Inc. As soon as he was ensconced at Milbank, Baity became the most powerful partner in the tax department.

In 1987, when the department chairmen were replaced by administrators, his position became formal and permanent. A lateral partner now held a position of power at Milbank.

In June 1987, shortly after Tufaro became a co-administrator of Milbank's litigation department, he finally had his way and recruited a high-profile litigator to the firm. Milbank even succeeded in attracting a household name—Thomas P. Puccio, the former Abscam prosecutor who had convicted six members of the

U.S. House of Representatives and one U.S. senator for bribery and other political corruption.

Tufaro and other litigation partners had made a list of potential laterals and then hired a headhunter to contact candidates. Puccio, a partner at Stroock & Stroock & Lavan, was not a litigator in the Milbank mold. Inside and outside the courtroom he was flamboyant. He fancied himself a celebrity of sorts and constantly dropped the names of friends, ranging from network anchormen to politicians. More significantly, Puccio had made his name in white-collar criminal law and not in complex civil litigation, the area Milbank aspired to develop.

Nevertheless, Tufaro, Connick, Brandow and Russell Brooks were impressed with him. Puccio, they believed, would be a counterbalance to the modest, self-effacing approach of Milbank's litigation team. He also would undoubtedly bring attention to the firm. "He knows people all over the city—he's constantly in touch with people," said Tufaro, "and personally I thought this was a very important quality to bring into this department." Milbank hoped that Puccio would bring in civil as well as criminal cases, but the firm was willing to take the risk that he would continue to attract primarily white-collar work.

Puccio had been impressed with Milbank's pitch and its litigators even though he had previously known almost nothing about them. This time, Milbank had been eager and ready to cut a deal. The partners told Puccio that they were not on the "short list" of New York's litigation departments and wanted his help to turn the department around. "They were interested in somebody to do something exciting—to be involved in building a litigation department," Puccio explained.

"What Milbank needs in litigation is a couple of major cases—maybe a great result that gets publicized," said Puccio. "What really puts you on the map is success in a high-profile case—that's the only way." He joined Tufaro and Connick as co-administrators of the department.

Reilly was not impressed with Puccio and his theories about developing Milbank's litigation practice. His feelings were well known to his partners, and he remained on the sidelines when Puccio was brought into the firm. He was convinced that he would ultimately be proven correct about glitzy litigation laterals. If the firm attracted good corporate business, he maintained, litigation would follow.

Puccio did bring in some newsworthy work. In 1988, he generated roughly $2 million in fees when he represented boxing manager Bill Clayton in his contract dispute with Mike Tyson. Clayton switched firms after he and Puccio disagreed over the cost of the legal services. ("Oh good," said one young Milbank partner who winced at the thought of Clayton's name alongside those of Chase and the Rockefellers on the firm's client rosters.) Puccio also represented investor John A. Mulheren, Jr., charged with securities fraud and other improprieties, as well as threatening to shoot convicted arbitrageur Ivan F. Boesky. As time went on, however, it seemed that Reilly was at least partly right. Puccio's arrival had worked no magic at the firm. The major victory he sought continued to be a distant hope. (In 1990 Mulheren was convicted of one count of conspiracy and three counts of securities fraud. The jury deadlocked on twenty-six other counts.) And Puccio didn't seem able to make the leap from generating criminal to complex civil litigation. "The opportunities haven't materialized the way I thought it would happen," acknowledged Tufaro. He nevertheless insisted that Puccio's energy, insight, and new perspective was a plus that would eventually pay off for Milbank.

Although Puccio said he was busy, Reilly liked to imply that Puccio's rainmaking efforts were less than successful. The two senior litigators "had their bumps," as Tufaro put it. "It's hard for Ed to give Tom a chance," he said. The tension sometimes bubbled up into disagreements over lawyer assignments and even case strategy.

But to the outside world it appeared that a "gale of fresh air" had hit Milbank, Tweed, as *Business Week* proclaimed in the summer of 1987. The magazine reported that "Milbank no longer disdains change," and went on to say that the firm's acquisition spree signified an awakening at the old-line Wall Street firm. Highlighted were Puccio and Alice Young, who had also just joined the firm as a partner.

Young had practiced at Coudert Brothers, and had been recruited in 1981 by Graham & James, a major San Francisco firm, to start its New York office. She was then only thirty-one years old, and was becoming known as a star among the New York lawyers struggling to develop an Asian clientele. As her practice grew at the small New York office, she decided she needed more backup. "My clients were telling me that they very much wanted me to expand into a lot of areas that for me would be difficult to service," she said.

So when Young was aggressively courted by Gewirtz and others at Milbank, she was receptive. "There are a lot of firms out there that talk big about what they're doing in Asia," said Young. "But it was clear that Milbank was superior." Although some New York lawyers were somewhat skeptical about the breadth of Young's practice, she was widely viewed as an asset to Milbank's international campaign. When she joined the firm in 1987, with a client roster that included NEC Home Electronics, U.S.A. Inc. and the Toyoda family, which founded the company that makes Toyota cars, there was even some talk in the legal community and press that she had replaced the luster that Milbank had lost with Shapiro.

Milbank's commitment to bringing in laterals was tested in 1987 and 1988 when it opened and cultivated its Los Angeles office. The partnership had revisited the decision to open the branch several times in 1986. Late that year, when the partnership finally voted to open the office in Los Angeles, the decision seemed almost anticlimactic. The partners were distracted by the unhappy departures of colleagues; the Los Angeles office had been on the agenda for so long that its launch

seemed to be a foregone conclusion. Only a few partners, including Reilly, declined to raise their hands in
favor of the plan.

It had always been assumed that Worenklein would
spend much of his time in Los Angeles when the office
opened. That turned out to be unnecesssary. Milbank
already had a Los Angeles lateral ready to head the
office. Guido R. Henry, Jr., known as Guy, a partner at
O'Melveny & Myers, one of his city's preeminent law
firms, had specialized in representing New York investment banks in transactions on the West Coast. About
a year before Henry was finally invited into the Milbank
partnership, he had been approached by a West Coast
headhunter working on the firm's behalf. In the past he
had rebuffed the overtures of New York firms seeking
a Los Angeles beachhead, but "as a kick," he had agreed
to meet with Milbank partners. In January 1986 he had
dinner at the Four Seasons in New York with Forger
and Worenklein, and over time he met with Logan and
Lilley as well. Still no offer came. Milbank was too ab-
sorbed with overhauling its management and compensation system to focus on opening a Los Angeles branch.
"It was emotionally tiring to kind of get interested and
then have it drag out and then nothing would happen,"
Henry said.

In October 1986, Henry flew from San Francisco,
where he was working on a merger, to Los Angeles to
meet with Worenklein and Brandow. The two partners
were finally prepared to make Henry an offer and he
was ready for a change. At O'Melveny he was one of

many corporate partners, but at Milbank he would be in a position to manage and create something. "I never wanted to be a back-office person," he said.

In early 1987 Henry moved into space sublet from Skadden, which had outgrown the office. At first it was almost eerie. Among rows of vacant offices were only a few Milbank lawyers, including lateral tax partner John Baity, whose Los Angeles clients were temporarily keeping him busy on the West Coast. Milbank's strategy was simple. Henry would try to develop a financial-services–based practice. During the office's first year he would recruit strong laterals in the corporate-finance, real estate, banking, and bankruptcy areas.

His first days at Milbank were sometimes worrisome. Former deputy secretary of state Warren M. Christopher, who ran O'Melveny, had seemed shocked but gracious when Henry told him he was leaving. The firm had gone on the defensive, however, and tried to prevent clients and other lawyers from following Henry. Other Los Angeles firms also went after Henry's clients.

Soon, however, the young office found its way. Executive committee member Floyd Brandow, only several years from retirement, volunteered to temporarily move to Los Angeles. Several younger New York partners, including new banking partner Katherine J. Moore, who had worked with Logan and Worenklein, bankruptcy partner David Frauman, and tax and trusts-and-estates partner Jonathan G. Blattmachr emigrated to the West Coast.

Henry was also able to bring in new partners from some of Los Angeles's better known firms. Thomas L.

Harnsberger, a former Latham & Watkins partner, joined to start a real estate practice; Richard J. Stone left the Los Angeles office of Sidley & Austin to launch a litigation group; and Edwin F. Feo and Ted Obrzut left Lillick, McHose & Charles to help build the bankruptcy department. In 1988, Eric Schunk, Henry's protégé at O'Melveny, was lured to Milbank with a promise of partnership.

By the end of 1987 the office had nine partners and nineteen associates; the firm had hoped to have two more partners in place by that point. In 1987, the office broke even—if one excluded payments to the Los Angeles partners—and in 1988 it made money even after distributions to partners. That year, Milbank's West Coast operation grew to about 55 lawyers, and it became the second largest New York–firm branch office in Los Angeles, after Skadden. The branch threatened to outgrow the sublet from Skadden, and made a new deal for space that could eventually accommodate almost 200 lawyers. Henry expected the office to grow at the rate of 7 or 8 percent a year and reach about 75 lawyers by the end of 1990. He and his team had advised more than 200 clients, including Dean Witter Reynolds Inc., First Boston, and Security Pacific Corporation. Chase and Citibank were also among the clients of Milbank west.

Milbank continued to try to build on its strength in Los Angeles—it wanted to be known for its financial-services expertise. But Henry felt that he lacked a strong Milbank banking partner on the West Coast. "I told Alex Forger we needed to clone Frank [Logan]," said Henry.

"I had used him by way of example." Henry tried to recruit other New York banking partners, never expecting that Logan would make the move.

But Forger approached Logan with the idea. "He worked on Frank for six months," said Henry. Los Angeles was such a big commitment, and such an important part of Milbank's future, Forger believed, that it was worth the sacrifice of the head of the Chase relationship in New York. He wanted to transplant Milbank's culture to the West Coast. "It *is* Milbank when you get someone like Frank Logan out there," Forger said.

For Logan, who had "spent thirty-four very happy, energetic years on Wall Steet," the Los Angeles move was indeed a sacrifice. At first, he had viewed the move as a silly idea. But as the firm's entreaties became more persistent, he began to change his mind. Logan and his wife took a vacation and decided to do it. "There's no return ticket," said Logan. Since he believed so strongly in the principles that had taken the firm to Los Angeles, he said, "Why not put a shoulder to the wheel?

"Maybe it's a good idea to have a link with the old fogies, of which I am a card-carrying member," he said. Logan passed the California bar exam, started wearing striped shirts, and in 1989 set about trying to build Milbank's West Coast international-finance practice. Henry and the rest of Milbank west were jubilant.

Logan continued to be co-administrator of the banking department, but he relinquished to Frank Puleo the post he had inherited from Roy Haberkern. He and others at Milbank had spoken with Chase general counsel Edward Shaw and president Thomas Labrecque before he had made his decision to move to Los Angeles. "I would not have come out here if those conversations hadn't gone as well as they did," Logan said. And so Puleo assumed responsibility for the Chase relationship with the consent of Chase's executives.

"We were very much part of the Chase family and I lived in that world for many years," said Logan, shortly after he arrived in Los Angeles. "To be out of that now is very odd, I admit."

Never before in Milbank's history could responsibility for Chase have been switched so easily. "The job of the Chase relationship point man has changed over time in a natural and positive way," said Puleo. Years before he had had no vision of what Chase's in-house department would become. The bank's decision to build a strong, high-quality legal staff, Puleo said, "was right for the bank and in many ways for Milbank too."

Milbank had once again twisted itself out of shape to preserve its collegiality and the relationships between its partners. But this time the firm's goals of growth and diversification were at the heart of its decision. "Frank Logan's move to the West Coast . . . has brought closer ties between [the New York and Los Angeles] offices than could have been imagined," said the executive committee in its report to the partnership in January 1989. Logan's move, "achieved without significant loss of position or momentum in New York, stands out among the most important recent achievements of the Firm—both in what it does for the Firm and what it says about the Firm."

EPILOGUE

IN MID-1988, MIL-
bank's executive committee appointed a committee to
come up with a strategic plan for the firm. Forger believed that Milbank's first phase of growth and diversification was drawing to a close. The firm had been
steadied and it was time to set new priorities and goals.

It made sense for Worenklein, as chief visionary, to
assume the chairmanship of the planning committee.
Lilley, Cooke, and Tufaro were among its other members. They hired a management consultant in 1988 to

help guide them, and set out to draft a "mission statement" that would define the partners' business goals for the firm.

Worenklein set a full agenda for his group. He wanted to mull every question the firm would face over the coming years—new offices, the quality of the lawyers' professional life, areas of practice, women's issues, and governance. "This group is examining us from stem to stern," said Forger happily. "It's as if we had a think tank."

The planning committee was armed with some sobering information. Tufaro, as chairman of the firm's client-relations committee, had previously commissioned another consulting firm, Zand Morris & Associates, to do a marketing report. The consultants interviewed people at large companies, some of which were Milbank clients, about how they chose law firms. Without telling respondents that they'd been hired by Milbank, the consultants asked for the participants' impressions of about ten major New York law firms, including Milbank and Skadden, Arps.

According to Worenklein, it turned out that Milbank was perceived in the survey as being "content with our position in the world." The participants in the survey did not think that Milbank was interested in marketing or bringing in new clients. "They were really responding to a Milbank that was long past. They went with the old image—white-shoe," said Worenklein. Milbank had changed its image of itself, but it had not conveyed the change to potential clients.

The study also showed that Milbank's strengths were still perceived to be in the banking and financial-services areas, and to a lesser degree in the international arena. Some of its other developing areas of expertise had not made a strong impression on the outside world. The executives who responded also connected the firm with Chase and the Rockefellers. "Our association with Chase and the Rockefellers was more negative than positive," said Tufaro. "It didn't give us sufficient independence."

Perhaps most disconcerting to Worenklein was the realization that potential clients were not looking for "quality and integrity" when choosing their counselors. Milbank had always prided itself on its technical superiority—but, the partners learned from the study, companies simply assumed they would find those attributes in any major law firm they hired. Superior work product could no longer be used as an effective selling point. Worenklein called it "a revolutionary conclusion."

In fact, executives were looking for entrepreneurial lawyers who took initiative and participated fully in their clients' business and made a discernible impact on transactions. Worenklein still believed that, to make that kind of impact, Milbank had to be able to do the kind of transactions that had the biggest effect on a company's future—mergers and acquisitions. Years before he had waged an unsuccessful campaign to convince his partners that Milbank belonged in M&A. But in 1988 and early 1989, his partners listened. Milbank had become preeminent in the banking arena at a time when commercial banks were no longer as important as invesment banks. "We achieved our objective at a time [when] that objective became less important," said Worenklein.

Forger now also believed the firm needed to turn its attention to building an M&A practice. "We have to be recognized as a player," he said. "We believe that's important for a lot of reasons." In a preliminary way, the planning committee discussed targeting laterals with solid M&A experience. These recruits would be expensive, but this time Milbank would not be encumbered by lockstep.

Worenklein's committee moved on to other issues. They concluded that the firm's international effort had been successful but looked ahead at new possibilities in Europe, where the European Community would unite its markets in 1992. They talked of the need to view further national expansion "opportunistically." And they discussed the need for interdepartmental cooperation and interdisciplinary practice groups structured along product lines.

As an outgrowth of the committee's work, Forger set up a new committee to study new changes in lockstep and the possibility of developing a bonus plan to reward partners for extraordinary short-term performance. "Now there is a willingness to consider incentives and the weapons that are available to implement the plans," he explained. There "has to be more leeway than we have now."

Finally, the committee considered the intangibles of law practice. They talked about the diversity of lawyers'

backgrounds and the need to make Milbank more hospitable to women and minorities. They mulled Milbank's
obligation to society and the less fortunate. "We are not
a trade or business. We are a profession," Forger liked
to remind his partners. He called his reminder "a hys-
terical note from the past."

In late 1989, as Worenklein and his group came
closer to composing a mission statement, the world
changed dramatically. That fall, as the stock market
plunged and the junk-bond market collapsed, it appeared that the legal profession's ascent to ever-stunning
economic heights might stall. Mergers dried up and even
lawyers at Skadden, Arps and Wachtell, Lipton started
going home earlier. The mood in Wall Street and midtown firms turned from haughty to somber. Worenklein,
however, was optimistic. American corporations, laden
with debt and uncompetitive, would have to restructure.
What firm was better poised to take on that kind of
challenge than Milbank? Worenklein argued. Milbank's
banking, bankruptcy, and financial expertise was bound
to make it a major player in the 1990s. Milbank still
needed a stronger M&A capability to round out its practice, but if the firm marketed aggressively and was op-
portunistic, it could take advantage of the downturn.

After over a year of work, in late 1989, the planning
committee presented a draft of the mission statement to
the executive committee. The two groups debated
whether the statement should emphasize Milbank's financial services bent or its aspirations as a mainstream
corporate firm. Though Puleo argued that the firm
should "lead with [its] strengths and stay with it," and

many agreed, members of both groups were equally committed to doing what was necessary to ensure that Milbank became competitive with other large corporate firms. They coined the phrase "leading corporate transactions" as a catch-all for M&A, restructurings and other kinds of deals that would affect the structure and direction of major companies in the murky 1990s.

The executive committee decided to defer on one issue Worenklein's group had raised. The planners believed that Milbank and other large firms would have to eventually revamp their partner/associate structure. Not every lawyer could be made a partner. In the 1980s, Milbank and other large firms had come up with "senior attorney" programs to try to keep talented, but sometimes passed-over, associates; but most law-firm managers felt that this modest change did not go far enough to provide a realistic alternative career path for good lawyers. Forger, Puleo, and Brandow were unwilling to tackle the issue immediately, and set it aside for further study.

As the mission statement was finalized, Forger pushed for a retreat to present the final product to the partnership. Tufaro thought it was unnecessary. The mission statement, he believed, set out broad goals. It would not change the partners' day-to-day life and it was not very controversial. But Forger insisted. If the partners developed a consensus on the plan, he believed, they would commit themselves to pursuing the goals set out as individuals and as an institution. A partners' retreat was set for March 31.

Many partners, however, considered a firm election

scheduled for right before the retreat to be more of a bellwether of the mood of the partnership. Floyd Brandow's term on the executive committee was expiring. He was approaching retirement and would not stand for reelection.

Since its first election in 1986, Milbank had revamped its unwieldy election process. A nominating committee interviewed partners and nominated two candidates to fill Brandow's spot on the committee. Lilley and Worenklein were put on the slate. Most partners believed that it didn't matter much which partner won. Both were respected practitioners and progressive managers. But there were several crucial differences. Worenklein, who in 1989 was responsible for at least $15 million in business, was still considered to be a catalyst for change. Many of his predictions, once scoffed at, had come to pass. Milbank did indeed have almost 500 lawyers. It was in Los Angeles. It had hired laterals and significantly diversified its practice. In 1989 its revenues were $187.7 million, and its profits per partner were $665,000. "His enthusiasm is infectious but he has this naïve streak that drives a number of us crazy," said Tufaro. "He provides vision and not discipline."

Lilley's outlook was considered to be more practical. He did provide discipline, "and a number of people framed it that way," said Tufaro. The two candidates, close colleagues, visited branch offices and fielded questions from their partners. Not all the partners were as optimistic about the future as Worenklein. Like big-firm lawyers all over the country, Milbank partners were worried. Milbank and other firms had even begun asking associates who were marginal performers to leave earlier than they had in the past. It was unclear whether the partners' insecurity would translate into a mandate for Lilley's cautious outlook or Worenklein's enthusiasm. Puleo thought it was a toss-up. Tufaro believed that as the election drew near the partnership shifted toward Worenklein.

No drama accompanied Milbank's election in March 1990. Partners sent in their ballots by interoffice mail and a committee headed by Jackson counted the votes, without the benefit of Price Waterhouse's assistance. Worenklein won with roughly 60 percent of the vote. Puleo saw the outcome as "a vote for continuing the process of change that the firm has been going through—perhaps at an increasing rate."

Forger tried to control his pride, but he couldn't help seeing Worenklein's election as the culmination of Milbank's cultural revolution. Milbank had cleared a hurdle, and its radical had become a member of the establishment.

A week later the partnership held a day-long retreat in a Chase auditorium and discussed the planning committee's mission statement. There was little vociferous debate. Forger, Worenklein, and the rest of the executive and planning committees had finally developed a strong consensus for change and a forward-looking strategy for the firm. At the end of the day, almost every partner raised his or her hand in support of the mission statement. It was not revolutionary, but it was a reaffirmation that Milbank wanted to be a contender among the country's strongest firms as it moved toward the next century and a younger generation took control of the firm.

> Our mission is to be a major contributor to the success of our clients and to be internationally recognized as one of the top tier of the nation's most prominent and successful law firms, preeminent in financial services and outstanding in leading corporate transactions and in each other area in which we practice. In pursuing this mission we will build on our traditions of excellence and integrity to serve a broader base of Milbank clients, to be a creative and vigorous force in the legal world, to help shape the profession and the law, and to contribute to the betterment of society.

Worenklein was pleased with the partnership's rousing support for the mission statement, but he knew there was a lot of hard work and painful decisions ahead of the executive committee. "It tells us where we have to end up," he said. "Everything else is details."

INDEX